Living Through History

THE EDWARDIAN ERA

GEOFFREY TREASE

B.T. Batsford Ltd London

ACKNOWLEDGMENTS

The Author and Publishers would like to thank the following for their kind permission to reproduce copyright illustrations: BBC Hulton Picture Library, figures 35, 43, 47 and 54; Elgar Foundation, figure 14; Mary Evans Picture Library, figures 10, 12, 13 and 41; GLC Photo Library, figure 26; Huntingdon Library, figure 23; Imperial War Museum, figures 21, 22 and 60; Labour Party, figure 27; Mandel Archive, figures 3, 4, 9, 18, 24 and 25; Raymond Mander and Joe Mitchenson Theatre Collection, figures 40 and 42; Mansell Collection, figures 1, 2, 5, 6, 7, 8, 17, 20, 28, 29, 30, 31, 32, 33, 34, 38, 39, 44, 45, 48, 49, 50, 55, 57, 58 and 59; Museum of London, figure 56; National Portrait Gallery, figures 19, 51, 52 and 53; National Trust, figures 15 and 16; Newham College, figure 36; University of Leeds, figure 11; Mrs Julia Vinogradoff, figure 46; Frank Wells (Weidenfeld Archives), figure 37. The pictures were researched by Patricia Mandel.

Cover illustrations
The colour illustration on the front cover shows Edwardian ladies and gentlemen enjoying the fresh air of a mountain resort; the black and white photograph shows the arrest of a Suffragette; the portrait is of David Lloyd George (*all three courtesy of the Mansell Collection*).

Frontispiece
Edward VII and Queen Alexandra at The Duchess of Wellington's Ball at Apsley House, 1908 (*Mansell Collection*).

Typeset by Tek-Art Ltd, West Wickham, Kent
Printed in Great Britain by
R J Acford
Chichester, Sussex
for the publishers
Batsford Academic and Educational,
an imprint of B.T. Batsford Ltd,
4 Fitzhardinge Street
London W1H 0AH

ISBN 0 7134 4919 5

CONTENTS

LIST OF
ILLUSTRATIONS

A GOLDEN AGE?

The Edwardian era began, very neatly, with the new century. After much public argument the Astronomer Royal had ruled that the twentieth century properly started not with the year 1900 but on 1 January 1901. Only three weeks later, on 22 January, Queen Victoria died after a reign of 63 years and her son was proclaimed King as Edward VII.

The end of the Edwardian period, however, is not usually dated by the King's death on 6 May 1910. Life continued very much the same under George V, a staid and conscientious

man with no taste for change. What ended the Edwardian era was the outbreak of the First World War (then called the Great War) in the summer of 1914. So historians commonly take these years together, 1901-1914, using "Edwardian", like "Regency", in a slightly wider sense.

There are many misconceptions about the period. It is often looked upon with romantic nostalgia as an age of elegance and security. Even the weather is said to have been better then, though this idea seems to have been dispelled by study of the meteorological records and to have been based on one or two memorably fine summers.

Was it a golden age? Nobody at the time seemed to think so, but it was natural, after the shocks and sufferings of the Great War, for older people to look back and imagine that it had been. This was particularly true of the upper and middle classes, whose supremacy had been shattered for ever. For many of the working-class population the pre-war years had been not only "the good old days" but also, in many respects, "the bad old days".

For the prosperous part of the nation it had been an age of unbelievably low income tax and unlimited cheap labour. Never again would standards of service be so high – and eagerly pressed upon any one who could pay. The railway platforms were thronged with willing porters and a boy from the bookstall would bring your newspaper to the carriage window. The streets were clean and tidy, thanks to an army of sweepers – much needed when horse-drawn traffic was still more common than petrol-driven. Shopkeepers and their assistants were respectful, sometimes to the point of being servile – and purchases were commonly delivered by van or at least by a boy on a bicycle. Great houses kept a host of servants, a middle-class villa might employ several, and even a quite modest householder (asserting his middle-class status with starched white collar and cuffs and a bowler

1 Triumphant welcome for volunteers returning from South Africa. Popular hysteria disguised the truth that it had been a hollow victory in a war that many people felt should never have been fought.

2 This period is rather inaccurately remembered as one of perpetual splendid summers. But certainly, when the sun did shine, regattas and other outdoor functions had an elegance that was never to be recaptured.

hat) would stretch his small salary to cover the cost of a maid.

Out of such circumstances was born the legend of "Edwardian elegance". And there was truth in the legend – there *was* elegance, easy enough when wealth and unlimited labour are available. Balls and banquets, regattas and race-meetings, naval reviews and nights at the opera were never more brilliant than in those years. The King loved pleasure – he brought a new gaiety to society after the drabber decades of his mother's long widowhood. He loved uniforms – and beautiful women, extravagantly dressed. So fashion flowered. True, society had not always waited patiently for the old Queen's passing – there had been the "Naughty Nineties" – but now at last the restraints were really removed. It is appropriate that the symbol of opulence, the Ritz Hotel, opened in 1906.

But there was the other side of the medal.

Unlimited labour implied the constant shadow of insecurity for the poorer half of the nation. Loyal and efficient service *was* often given by people who took a pride in their work and genuinely liked – indeed sometimes loved – those who employed them. But not seldom it sprang from fear of dismissal, which could be suffered for the smallest fault or even at the mere whim of a cantankerous master or mistress. Too often the servant's respectful face masked a boiling hatred or contempt. In most cases the relationship would, of course, be much less emotional and one of neither love nor loathing. And what was true of domestic service applied in shops and offices and factories. There were good bosses and bad, but a job of any kind was the first essential.

Looking at old photographs – smiling at the elaborate formal clothes and the antiquated vehicles – we may feel that this period is remote and irrelevant to us. It is not so. Closer study shows that these bygone Edwardians faced, in an earlier form, most of the problems we ourselves have to cope with today.

Unemployment, bad housing and malnutrition were rife. There were strikes and violent demonstrations. There was the

3 Poorer folk had their own cause to hope for fine weather. Here, photographed by Jack London in 1902, are homeless women who had to sleep out on the public benches of Spitalfields Gardens, close to the fabulously wealthy "City", financial heart of the Empire.

struggle for sex-equality – won today so far as Parliamentary voting is concerned, but still unfinished in several other fields. There was bitter controversy over Ireland, though that country was still part of the United Kingdom and the "Irish question" was different in form. There was fierce argument over the powers of the House of Lords. There were "immigrants" – especially Russian and Polish Jews fleeing from persecution under the Tsar and settling mainly in London's East End – and there were "emigrants", who saw a poor future for themselves at home in Britain and sought better opportunities in the United States or the developing dominions of the Empire. And there was the fear of a coming war, very real to a thoughtful minority, though it seldom troubled the mass of the nation, who were surprised and indignant when it overwhelmed them in 1914. In all these matters there are informative comparisons and contrasts that help us to understand our own time.

Reading about the dozen men and women depicted in these pages we may also feel that Edwardian Britain – and certainly Edwardian London – was a very small world. Mostly these people, so varied in their lives, knew each other. The Conservative leader, Balfour, will be seen chatting with H. G. Wells at dinner, or laughing with the extraordinary Lady Ottoline at one of her bohemian parties. Sylvia Pankhurst, as a rebellious art student, will be running up the stairs to Keir Hardie's flat to pour out her troubles to the founder of the Labour Party – and Bernard Shaw will be sitting down with Hardie to draft together a political programme. There was time for long

4 Upper and middle classes enjoyed a high degree of personal service. Conditions varied enormously. This head housemaid of 19 and under-housemaid of 16, photographed on a day off in Scarborough about 1908, look anything but downtrodden.

conversations and letter-writing, above all time for friendships.

The personality of the King must not be underrated. He came to the throne with a difficult task. He had to follow a much-loved and venerated sovereign – who, as his mother, had disliked and disapproved of him. She had firmly kept him out of public affairs so that, at almost 60, he was taking over an important and complicated function for which he was utterly untrained. His biographer, Christopher Hibbert tells of the zest with which he plunged into the work:

He would ask question after question, interrupt the answers with his quick, "Yes . . . yes . . . yes", give orders, scribble notes on bits of paper in his scarcely legible hand-writing, and then stand in front of the fire with one of his immense cigars between his teeth, "looking wonderfully like Henry VIII, only better tempered". The impression he gave Lord Esher was "that of a man, who, after long years of pent-up action, had suddenly been freed from restraint and revelled in his liberty". (*Edward VII, A Portrait*)

Nor was it just a question of learning to carry on things as before. Even the sovereign had to adapt himself to the changes of the new century. Victoria's life had spanned a gulf stretching back to Georgian times when monarchs had still exerted considerable power. To some extent the strong-willed little Queen had managed to keep things that way. But her son had to reign over a twentieth-century democracy with ministers who tried to use him as a rubber-stamp to their decisions. As his secretary, Lord Knollys, protested, their perfunctory reports "made an absolute fool of the King". He said:

There is no use in ministers *liking* the King if he is treated like a puppet.

Edward had to make the transition with dignity, and for all his huffing and puffing, his tantrums and prejudices, he did it remarkably well.

He liked people and had a talent for projecting himself. There had long been complaints because the old Queen had secluded herself at Windsor and Balmoral, so that for all the expense of monarchy the nation got no colourful pageantry in return. Edward restored the State opening of Parliament, abandoned for 40 years. He was seen at the theatre and other public gatherings – not least at race-meetings. In the last year of his reign he was able to lead in his third Derby winner, Minoru, to deafening shouts of 'Good old Teddy!' from a multitude who loved a sportsman. He was hearty and affable with all, not standing on his dignity and so never losing it. Even the journalists loved him.

He was emphatically not intellectual. He loved drink and cigars, gargantuan meals and amorous affairs. As Prince of Wales he had been what was later to be termed a "playboy". As a conscientious King, he still contrived to enjoy himself. At the German spa of Marienbad in 1905 he fell in with the Liberal leader, Sir Henry Campbell-Bannerman, and found his company unexpectedly agreeable. The M.P. was bidden to lunch or dinner almost every day, and complained afterwards:

I got so mixed up with the King's incessant gaieties, for which his energy and appetite are alike insatiable, that it was no rest or holiday for me. Thus when at last he was gone my doctor ordered me to bed and absolute rest for forty-eight hours.

5 The sport-loving King was especially popular with racegoers. His horses had three times won the classic event, the Derby. Here he is seen with the third winner, Minoru, in 1909.

Although his prime ministers (and Campbell-Bannerman was soon to be one of them) kept him from interfering with their policies, Edward did exert a quiet influence – and express less quiet opinions – of his own. He backed Fisher in building up the navy and Haldane in his army reforms, and he would question Asquith anxiously about defence preparations. He made plain his disapproval of Lloyd George and about Suffragettes he waxed furious. A sovereign could still speak his mind with a freedom impossible today.

In foreign affairs his geniality and European network of royal family relationships made him diplomatically useful, though he abominated his German nephew, Kaiser Wilhelm II. It is debatable how far he deserved his nickname, "Edward the Peacemaker", for we now know more about the complex factors involved in the war that was soon to break out, but he did his best and people at the time certainly credited him with enormous influence. The American ambassador told his President in 1907 that Edward was "the greatest mainstay of peace in Europe", and the Italian Foreign Minister declared:

He is, and this one cannot deny, the arbiter of Europe's destiny, the most powerful personal factor in world policy. And, as he is for peace, his overall approach will serve above all to maintain harmony between the nations.

He was also for the British Empire, which was still expanding and seemed full of splendid possibilities. Soon after his accession this was reflected in the addition to his title of the words "and of the British Dominions beyond the Seas". But the future was to prove very different from his dream.

If not truly a golden age, the Edwardian era was at least a brief interlude of peace and promise between two disastrous wars. It came in during the weary conflict in South Africa; and it went out, like a snuffed candle, when the grey-uniformed tide of German armies began to wash round the frontier fortresses of Belgium.

THE PATRIOTS

What do we mean by "patriot"? Ask any group – and prepare for an argument.

Does it imply loving our country and being proud of it, yet admitting the fine points of others? Does it mean a fanatical emotion, "my country right or wrong"? Or a blind loyalty to established institutions, from the Crown downwards, and a hostility to change?

Edwardian Britain was strong in patriotic feeling. It took many forms – from the sublimity of Elgar's music, inspired by his native countryside, to the bellowed jingoistic choruses of the music halls; and from the sincere ideals of statesmen to the hysteria of mobs raging against pro-Boer sympathizers at the start of the period and harmless London shopkeepers with German-sounding names at the end.

The individuals studied in the next few pages have been grouped as "patriots" because that word, though capable of different shades of meaning, conveys what they had in common – a pride in their country and a general acceptance of the way in which it was run.

If we try to see things with Edwardian eyes we must admit that they had much to be proud of. It was natural that they should have grown a little smug. Britain's prestige was immense throughout the world. She was constantly – if sometimes reluctantly – enlarging her vast empire. She had long ago pioneered the Industrial Revolution and become "the workshop of the world". She exported not only her goods but her inventive skills to every continent. True, she was losing this absolute predominance – for a generation the United States and the new German Empire had been over-hauling her, but the man-in-the-street hardly realized that. British goods, British justice and British political freedom were genuinely admired abroad.

Although the British might speak romantically of their "breed", the "island race" and "Norman blood", they did not hold strict racial theories like those later preached by Hitler. They knew they were a mixed stock including many strains, from the ancient Celtic Welsh to the French Huguenots and many still more recent immigrants entering freely from other parts of Europe. What bound them together was really a common set of values, a respect for law and tradition, and a way of life untroubled by revolutions and invasions.

The idea of the Empire was fairly new. Many people had been against Queen Victoria's taking the title Empress of India in 1877. The planting of the flag in new territories, especially in Africa, was not popular with everybody. These critics were derided as "Little Englanders" by the extremer enthusiasts, who saw empire-building as a high mission and their own label, "imperialist", as nothing to apologize for. Most moderate people, in the middle, felt that a powerful Britain was a good thing for the world in general and especially as a keeper of the peace.

Human nature being what it is, the patriotism of the British cloaked widely differing characters and motives. There were the unscrupulous adventurers, speculators and swindlers, and there were the idealists. Between them lay the great mass of averagely decent people, who had to earn a living, who found careers overseas, but who also often found a further satisfaction in their service, beyond the mere salary and pension.

Two influences (hard for young people today to imagine) had contributed immeasurably in creating this attitude. One was the Victorian public school, inculcating moral values, a cult of leadership, and an idealistic conception of a Briton's role and responsibility abroad. The other (believe it or not) was the effect of the popular adventure story, devoured by girls as well as boys, in an era when there was neither television nor cinema. In particular G. A. Henty, author of countless books with titles like *By England's Aid, Held Fast for England* and *With Roberts to Pretoria*, inspired countless young people to enlist in the armed forces, to emigrate or to enter the Indian or Colonial Civil Services. Henty, it was said, did more to arouse a pride in the nation's history than all the schoolmasters put together.

No wonder that in 1914 young Rupert Brooke could write with sincerity in *The Soldier*:

If I should die, think only this of me:
    That there's some corner of a foreign field
That is for ever England.

It was not until several years later, when Brooke, along with millions of others, was dead – when indeed the Edwardian era itself was dead – that another poet, Wilfred Owen, could end his horrific description of a gas attack in *Dulce et Decorum Est*:

My friend, you would not tell with such high zest
To children ardent for some desperate glory,
The old Lie: *Dulce et decorum est*
Pro patria mori.

Sweet and seemly to die for one's country? There would be heroism again in the Second World War, and self-sacrifice, but the Edwardian brand of patriotism could never return.

Arthur James Balfour (1848-1930)

Edward VII was crowned on 9 August 1902 amid scenes of imperial pomp that were the high-water mark of Britain's power. He reigned over the first "world" empire since Rome, and a far vaster one, for now the whole world was known and a quarter of its land surface was covered by his dominions. But even on that day of most glittering show and splendour he could not delude himself that he was the most powerful man present. That man, inconspicuous among the robes and uniforms, the coronets and the plumed helmets, was the Prime Minister.

If it had not been for the King's recent emergency operation for appendicitis, suddenly postponing the coronation from 26 June, it would have been a different prime

7 Balfour takes his place as Prime Minister for the first time in 1902. He walks between his colleagues sitting on the Government front bench and the ornate dispatch-box at which they make their speeches.

minister. It would have been the ageing Lord Salisbury – the last peer to head a government – who died the following year. He had been waiting to resign until the South African War ended. When the coronation was postponed he waited no longer, but handed over to his trusted nephew, Arthur Balfour, already leading the Conservatives in the House of Commons and generally accepted as his obvious successor. Balfour took office on 12 July.

He was a paradoxical, enigmatic character. A foreigner might have expected Britain to be led, in this period, by an aggressive, iron-willed empire-builder, a sort of British Bonaparte or Bismarck. Instead, he would have seen a tall, willowy figure, lounging on the front bench in Parliament in a nearly horizontal attitude and reputed seldom to leave his bed until midday. The hot-headed young Winston Churchill had long ago told his mother that Balfour was a "languid, lazy, lack-a-daisical cynic, the unmonumental figurehead of the Conservative Party." He was notoriously indecisive. As someone said, "he nailed his colours to the fence". An odd choice of leader for the British Empire entering the twentieth century? It is worth inquiring deeper.

Balfour had certainly been lucky in birth and background. Through his mother, Lady Blanche, one of the historic Cecil family, he was related to half the aristocracy and a frequent guest in great ducal homes like Chatsworth and Blenheim Palace. He was rich: his father, a Scottish M.P., had died when he was a small boy, leaving him four million pounds and a 10,000-acre estate. Admittedly he had not distinguished himself at Eton, being what is now termed "a loner", fonder of country walks than cricket, perhaps because of poor sight. Schoolboys then were reluctant to wear spectacles. But once he reached Cambridge he became a good tennis-player and later a keen golfer.

Possibly those country walks had encouraged thinking. He was said to have had a better brain than any other politician of his period. Even the old Queen (whom he respected) had been a little in awe of him. The

8 July 1905: Balfour leaves the historic Downing Street house which in a few months he will quit for ever as Prime Minister. He has been a keen motorist for five years past, his love of speed causing him to buy new cars of ever-increasing horse-power.

new King (whom he privately did not much respect) disliked him. Edward loved shooting birds – by the thousand. Balfour, unlike most gentlemen, did not. Edward read little. Balfour read incessantly, in bed, in his bath, even as he shaved – science, philosophy, theology, detective-stories, anything but the newspapers. He was rare, unique even, among his contemporaries in his grasp of science. While they peppered their parliamentary speeches with Latin tags, he seldom made a classical reference. He preferred the future to the past, young company to old.

True, he got up late. But in those morning hours in bed he dealt with a formidable volume of work. The languidness was an illusion. So was the coldness, the aloofness that repelled the jovial King. Balfour in fact had immense charm, attracting the friendship of men and women alike. "He was the best talker I have ever known," said the novelist John Buchan. In her book, *More Memories*, the irrepressible Margot Asquith, explained that misleading coolness:

Arthur Balfour was born with perfect equilibrium, and an admirable temper and iron nerves. I have often seen him masterful, cool and collected in debates which aroused prolonged party fury in the House of Commons.

She recalled driving in his "motor" (he was an early and enthusiastic motorist), skidding down dangerous slopes and once crashing against a lorry in the dark. It is to be hoped that the lorry was stationary and unoccupied,

9 An earlier enthusiasm was the newly fashionable game of golf. At this date he was Chancellor of the Exchequer.

The Indefinite Article.

for "he never moved in his seat, and we continued our conversation as if nothing had occurred".

Margot was affected by Balfour's charm and at one time made determined efforts to marry him. Balfour was asked about a rumour that they were engaged. "No, that is not so," he said with his usual blandness, "I rather think of having a career of my own."

He never married. He was not so much cold as controlled, attracted to women but unwilling to surrender his independence. His unmarried sister Alice ran the house he had inherited, overlooking the Firth of Forth, and his younger brothers and their children were encouraged to treat it as their own home.

What was he like as Prime Minister? Behind that languid mask were an acute intelligence and a determined will. His immediate problem was to hold the Conservative Party together and to keep it in power. The party had been in office for some years and had lost much popularity owing to the bungling of the South African War. It was inwardly divided on issues like tariff reform, to give up Britain's tradition of free trade and impose duties to favour her own colonies. This was preached by the keen imperialists under the thrustful Birmingham business man Joseph Chamberlain, of whom Balfour spoke with his usual tolerant mildness.

Joe, though we all love him dearly, somehow does not absolutely or completely mix, does not form a chemical combination with us.

He had no illusions about the quality of other less able colleagues, remarking of one: "If he had a little more brains he would be a half-wit."

Winston Churchill, by now an M.P., proved an undependable supporter. Despite Winston's contemptuous comments years before, Jennie Churchill had approached Balfour for help in placing her son's first book, and he, with his usual generosity, had recommended it to his own literary agent and thereby assisted its publication. But such personal kindnesses are – quite properly – irrelevant to political disagreements. In 1904

the disgruntled Churchill crossed over to the Liberals, and, when he rose to make his next speech, amid cries of "Rat!" Balfour for once displayed his own feelings. Jennie Churchill recorded:

That detestable Arthur Balfour and his entire party got up and walked out of the House. What an insult from a Prime Minister! . . . I'll never speak to him again.

Balfour was clinging to power so that he could complete certain tasks that he thought vital for the country. The recent war had shown the army's dangerous weakness in artillery. It was now to be re-armed with a new quick-firing 18-pounder gun. He was anxious to finish that process or at least push it so far that, if the Liberals won the next election, it would be too late for them to abandon it. He wanted, too, to consolidate the Entente with France and to develop the Committee of Imperial Defence formed to meet the challenges of the new century.

He was also preoccupied with an education bill that he had largely drafted himself, and which was very dear to his heart. The state was already obliged to provide primary schools for all. Now it was to be equally responsible for secondary education. Forward-looking,

10 A constant diner-out and guest at upper-class house-parties, Balfour enjoyed a full social life – whether or not he shared in the current craze for ping-pong (as table tennis was then called) which was all the rage from 1899 to 1904.

11 Balfour early saw the importance of scientific education. This laboratory was at Leeds, one of the new universities created out of existing local colleges. About the same date, 1908, H.G. Wells's fictitious character Ann Veronica may be imagined in a similar setting in Kensington.

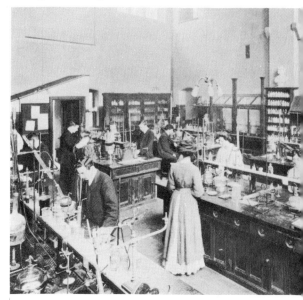

realizing the importance of scientific and technical training, Balfour wanted Britain to have a system able to meet the competition provided by Germany. He was also keenly interested in the establishment of new universities, which were developed out of earlier institutions at Liverpool (1903), Leeds (1904) and Sheffield (1905).

The appalling social conditions of his country did not loom large in his mind. He was too intelligent not to have been aware of the poverty and slums, though he probably saw little with his own eyes, dining out every evening in the great houses and clubs, motoring, golfing and "week-ending" at upper-class house-parties. It is said that he invented the British week-end, for, in his desire to get to the golf course, he altered the House of Commons timetable, so that it sat in the morning on Fridays and then adjourned early. Like many of his circle he was sorry for the poor and wanted to improve their lot, but, while other rich Tories assumed it could be done without any sacrifice of their own comforts and privileges, he was sceptical enough to fear that the gain of one class would mean loss for another.

Somehow he kept going until December, 1905, when the aggressive demands of the Chamberlain faction for tariff reform threatened a fatal split among the Conservatives. Balfour resigned. The King could only invite the Liberal leader, Sir Henry Campbell-Bannerman, to form a government – and Campbell-Bannerman, while accepting, could only call a general election for the New Year, since he had no majority of Liberal M.P.s to support him in the House. That "landslide" election swept the Liberal Party into power with a huge majority. Balfour actually lost his own seat, and, until a vacancy was arranged for him, could not even return to lead the opposition.

Speaking at Nottingham during the election Balfour had made a significant statement.

It is the duty of everyone to see that the great Unionist Party [i.e. Conservatives] shall still control, whether in power or whether in opposition, the destinies of this great Empire.

There was only one way in which this could be done – by the House of Lords, with its permanent Conservative majority, obstructing the decisions of a Liberal-dominated House of Commons. This is what was done, leading to the bitter constitutional struggles of the years that now followed, and causing the fiery Lloyd George to declare in 1908:

The House of Lords is not the watchdog of the constitution; it is Mr Balfour's poodle.

In 1911 Balfour gave up his leadership of the Conservatives, pleading ill-health, but the First World War brought him into action again as a prominent member of the Coalition Government, one of the four-man War Cabinet. Today he is chiefly remembered not for his heyday in the Edwardian period but for the Balfour Declaration of 1917, which led eventually to the establishment of a Jewish homeland, now the state of Israel.

Edward Elgar (1857-1934)

For many people Elgar's music has made him the very personification of Edwardian England. They point to the swelling confidence of that most familiar piece:

Land of Hope and Glory, Mother of the Free,
How shall we extol thee, who are born of thee?
Wider still and wider shall thy bounds be set;
God who made thee mighty, make thee mightier
  yet.

What they do not always realize is that these words were not written by the composer of the music, and that as the years went by he was acutely embarrassed by their jingoist flavour.

He had been asked to write music for Edward's coronation. At that date he had just achieved fame after years of depressing struggle. Works like his *Enigma Variations* and *The Dream of Gerontius* had shown that England had now a composer to be taken seriously. Elgar was as patriotic as anyone – he was happy to produce his *Coronation Ode* and his *Pomp and Circumstance* marches – but it was the new King who so liked one of the tunes that he asked for words to be set to it, to make it a national song. A. C. Benson supplied the words, the song became immensely popular – and it haunted Elgar ever afterwards.

It is not unfair, however, to consider him as essentially an Edwardian figure. Those were the years of his greatest reputation, when titles, decorations and honorary degrees were showered upon him. Most of his other first-rate work belongs to that period. Only the superb cello concerto came, like a late flowering, in 1919. Then came a fall from fashion, a neglect even more bitter than the lack of recognition he had suffered until he was over 40.

He had been born in simple circumstances. His father kept a music-shop in Worcester High Street, played the organ at the Roman Catholic church and rode round the big country houses on a thoroughbred horse, to tune the pianos of the "quality". Sometimes, as a little boy, Edward was taken on these rounds. Thus, through his father, he learned

12 Edward VII's coach passing the Horse Guards en route for his coronation in Westminster Abbey, 9 August 1902. One site of Elgar's genius responded grandly to such state occasions.

to love horses, and the mellow countryside of the Severn Vale and Malvern Hills, and the gracious atmosphere of the big mansions, and – above all – music.

Mr Elgar was well-mannered and "gentlemanly"; Mrs Elgar loved poetry and even wrote a little herself, but they had a big family and no money to spare. When Edward resolved on a career in music he could afford hardly any lessons, and certainly no full-time training. He was self-taught, mastering one instrument after another that he found in the shop – violin and viola, cello and bassoon – and, of course, the piano, and then, like his father, the organ.

He began to give music lessons. One of his pupils was a young woman – though older than himself – Alice Roberts, daughter of Major-General Sir Henry Roberts. She lived with her widowed mother in a fine house near Malvern and was driven over to her lessons there. After a time the family coachman is said to have remarked, "There's more in this than music – if you ask me!"

There was. When Lady Roberts died Alice moved into a room in Malvern. Soon she horrified her relatives by announcing her engagement to Elgar. She, a general's daughter! And *he*, a penniless music-teacher – whose father was "in trade"! But they could not stop her. One aunt struck Alice's name out of her will. Another thing that Elgar personifies is the relentless class feeling of the age.

Elgar was not a conspicuous rebel against it. Bitter though he might be about the snubs and slights of those years, he preferred – with Alice's guidance – to conform, to be absorbed and accepted by the upper class when success came to him, and to enjoy unashamedly a place among the privileged. Already in *Enigma* (1899) the "friends pictured within" are a genteel, cultured group. In 1904 he achieved a knighthood. In later years when a fellow composer hesitated about accepting the same honour Elgar urged him to do so. "No one in England," he declared cynically, "thinks anything of a musician unless he has a title."

Luckily he had the features and bearing to

13 Elgar in 1904, the year he was knighted, composing in his quiet study at the foot of the Malvern Hills.

match his new distinction. A young friend, Dorabella, nicknamed him "His Excellency", and many people thought he looked more like a general than a composer. Once he rebuffed a young journalist, saying that he never gave press interviews. The man wrote up their brief encounter none the less, and sent a copy. He had described Elgar as "aristocratic", which so delighted Lady Elgar that she responded with a warm invitation to luncheon at Hereford, where they now had a big house.

It was Christmas week, 1905, and the country was boiling up to that fateful General Election of January 1906. Later, in his book *Set Down in Malice*, C. F. Kenyon recalled how, as he ate and drank, his hostess told him that the Empire was going to the dogs.

Lady Elgar did not seem to wish to know to what particular party (if any) I belonged, but I quickly discovered that to confess myself a Radical would be to arouse feelings of hostility in her bosom. Radicals were the Unspeakable People. There was not one, I gathered, in Hereford. They appeared to infest Lancashire, and some had been heard of in Wales. . . .

What was the country coming to?

I did not allow Lady Elgar's rather violent political prejudices to interfere with my appetite, and she appeared to be perfectly satisfied with an occasional sudden lift of my eyebrows, and such ejaculations as: 'Oh, quite! Quite!', 'Most assuredly!' and 'Incredible!' If she thought about me at all – and I am persuaded she did not – she must have believed me also to be a Tory. After all, had not I called her husband 'aristocratic'?

Lady Elgar must have been horrified a week or two later when all the election results were known, for safe Tory seats had been lost everywhere, and the benches were filled with 377 Liberals and 53 of the new "Labour" representatives.

When Elgar himself, after luncheon, took his guest for a walk beside the River Wye, he was much more "reserved and non-

14 Elgar with his beloved bicycle, Mr Phoebus, on which he ranged the beautiful Worcestershire countryside. With the car still in its infancy the bicycle was, for Edwardians of all classes, the great liberating invention.

committal". His sympathies were traditional, even conventional, he was "for" the monarchy, the Empire, and the existing order of society, but his heart and mind were really set upon his music.

A year or two earlier, in an interview he had granted to the *Strand* magazine, he had good-temperedly defended the "musical crimes" – the tuneful works enjoyed by a wide public – of which the more serious critics were already accusing him.

Oh, you mean the *Cockaigne*, the *Coronation Ode* and the *Imperial March* especially? Yes, I believe there are a good many people who have objected to them. But I like to look on the composer's vocation as the old troubadours or bards did. In those days it was no disgrace to a man to be turned on to step in front of an army and inspire the people with a song. . . . I do know we are a nation with great military proclivities . . . I have some of the soldier instincts in me, and so I have written two marches of which, so far from being ashamed, I am proud.

Like most people at that time he had the Old Victorian assumptions – war was something that happened a long way off and was always won by the British. It was fought by gallant red-coated professionals, it did not touch the majority. They saw soldiers only on ceremonial parades or playing light music in the parks.

When war came nearer home, in 1914, Elgar's complacency was shattered as devastatingly as anyone's. He was too old himself to fight and he was spared the loss of sons – the Elgars had one daughter only – but he saw the decimation of the younger generation, including many musicians of promise he had known. Besides the human slaughter he was horrified by the sufferings of the horses he had loved since childhood: though the machine-gun had quickly made cavalry charges obsolete there were still thousands of horses going into battle to draw guns and supply waggons, and many were blown to pieces or hideously mutilated. Yet another cause for grief was that Britain was being forced to fight Germany – the country whose music had most influenced him, where his own musical genius had been first recognized when he was still little known in England, and where he had found so many friends.

Elgar realized before most people that the war had irrevocably swept away the old England he had known and loved. All his sensitivity and melancholy went into the grandly moving cello concerto, written during the first months of the peace. It expressed, he once said, "a man's attitude to life". It could also be described as a requiem for the vanished Edwardian world.

Rudyard Kipling (1865-1936)

As Elgar personified Edwardian patriotism in music, so – and even more markedly – did Kipling in literature.

The two men were alike in being individuals of genius who were not born into the conventional upper class. Kipling's connections were less humble than Elgar's – his "Uncle Ned" was the great Victorian painter, Sir Edward Burne-Jones, and his cousin, Stanley Baldwin, was later to be Prime Minister – but his father held a modest post as head of a new art school in Bombay, where Rudyard was born. He was sent "home", as small English children always were, for health reasons, spent some unhappy early years apart from his parents, and went to the Devon boarding school depicted in his book, *Stalky and Co.* – a "public school" but not one which conferred any great social prestige or moulded his original character into stereotyped prejudices. From school he went back to India, not as a soldier or administrator like other public schoolboys, but as a hardworking journalist on the *Civil and Military Gazette* at Lahore.

In many respects Elgar and Kipling were emphatic contrasts. Elgar, after his long, humiliating struggles, was a willing social conformer, delighted with the conventional honours that belatedly came his way. Kipling was lucky to win much earlier recognition, and, though he would accept honorary doctorates from universities and eventually the Nobel prize for literature, he would take nothing from the government. As early as 1895 Balfour had suggested that he be appointed Poet Laureate, but it was learnt that the 30-year-old writer would not be tempted by the honour, and he maintained that attitude all his life.

Elgar was seldom out of his beloved England: his patriotism was in his blood, instinctive, and his political interests were minimal. Kipling – apart from his chequered childhood and spartan schooldays – did not settle in England until 1896, and his patriotism had quite different, consciously political, roots.

Though his love of England is eloquently expressed in his poems it was surpassed by his feeling for the Empire – just as his pride in the English people seems concerned more with the Englishmen overseas than those at home. When Kipling spoke of the Empire he was no dewy-eyed sentimentalist. He knew the Empire as few others did.

India, above all. When he returned as a young newspaperman he added a fresh and varied experience to his childhood recollections. He went hither and thither among the people, Hindu and Muslim alike, able to talk freely with them in their own language as he reported everything from a village festival to a communal riot. Equally, he could talk to the rank-and-file British soldiers – so much so that, at 22, he was consulted by

the Commander-in-Chief about the real state of feeling among the troops. And in the select Punjab Club he could mingle with their officers and the civil servants – the administrators and lawyers, the key men in forestry, irrigation, health, railways.

No phrase has roused more derision than "the white man's burden" in his poem of the same name. What Kipling actually wrote was:

Take up the White Man's burden –
  And reap his old reward:
The blame of those ye better,
  The hate of those ye guard.

He knew the many faults of the British in India. He had seen some of them loved and respected, others fiercely criticized and vilified. He had no illusions. But he gave them credit for being generally honest and conscientious, doing worthwhile work that no one else was yet trained to do. He left India in 1889, yet he will be for ever specially associated with that country.

He returned only briefly to England. He visited South Africa, New Zealand, Australia and Canada, with calls at Rangoon, Singapore and Hong Kong. In South Africa he made friends with two imperialist politicians, Cecil

15 Kipling reading aloud to children on a liner bound for South Africa in 1902. He had a genius for story-telling to young and old alike, but his political influence is not to be underestimated.

Rhodes, after whom Zimbabwe was first named, and Alfred Milner, the British High Commissioner. Later, Rhodes provided him with a house on his estate at Capetown, and from 1900 to 1907 Kipling used it to escape the English winters. In Canada – also in the 1900s – his growing fame earned him the free use of a private railway coach. It could be attached to any train he chose, and enabled him to travel widely in the vast dominion.

Despite all this enthusiasm for the fast-developing Empire, it was an American he married. But so did many eminent Englishmen at this period, including Winston Churchill's father, and King Edward later encouraged the practice. Kipling's bride, Caroline Balestier, had already been described by her fellow-countryman, the novelist Henry James, as "remarkable in her force, acuteness, capacity and courage", and it was he who gave her away at "a dreary little wedding" just after the death of her brother. He could not understand Kipling's marrying her and would not forecast their future together. Of the bridegroom he wrote:

Kipling strikes me personally as the most complete man of genius (as distinct from fine intelligence) that I have ever known.

For all Henry James's forebodings, the marriage worked. The next four years, 1892-1896, were spent in Vermont and were among the happiest in Kipling's life. He loved America. But two things impelled him to leave: a dispute with a hard-drinking, outrageous brother-in-law, leading to court proceedings and painful publicity; and a wider, international dispute between Britain and the United States over the Venezuelan frontier, which – incredible though it may sound to us now – raised the possibility of an Anglo-American war.

So at last Kipling came back to England and made it his home. But, as he told Rhodes later, he found England "a stuffy little place, mentally, morally and physically". At first the Kiplings stayed in Torquay, "such a place as I do desire to upset by dancing through it with nothing on but my spectacles. Villas, clipped hedges and shaven lawns; fat old ladies . . ."

In 1902, however, they settled finally in the mellow old stone house, Bateman's at Burwash in Sussex, where visitors can still see his study very much as he left it. At last he could write with real enthusiasm:

Each to his choice, and I rejoice
    The lot has fallen to me
In a fair ground – in a fair ground –
Yea, Sussex by the sea!

But, before that, the Boer War had taken him to South Africa again. Always most sympathetic to the rank-and-file regular soldier, he had published in the *Daily Mail* one of his popular, slangy poems, "The Absent-minded Beggar". It caught the public imagination. It was reprinted, recited everywhere, sung to music by Sullivan. Kipling would not accept a penny for its use. Everything went into "The Absent-minded Beggar Fund" to provide comforts for the troops. The poem produced altogether a quarter of a million pounds, an enormous sum in 1900.

Kipling went out and toured hospitals and camps to make sure that the money reached the men it was intended for. He was then asked to help with the production of an army

16 "Bateman's", the house (built in 1634) with which Kipling fell in love at sight, living in it until his death. It overlooks Pook's Hill, and is kept by the National Trust much as he left it.

newspaper. This enabled him, though not a soldier, to be an eye-witness of the fighting.

That war, with its humiliating disasters and notorious mismanagement, jolted the nation. To Kipling, on the spot, it was an even greater shock. He wrote in *The Times:*

Let us admit it fairly, as a business people
  should,
We have had no end of a lesson: it will do us no
  end of good . . .
So the more we work and the less we talk the
  better results we shall get –
We have had an Imperial lesson; it may make us
  an Empire yet!

Had the British gone soft? If they had fared so poorly against Boer farmers how would they withstand a huge European army? Back home, Kipling formed a local branch of the Navy League and a company of volunteers, building them a drill hall. He had seen British soldiers picked off at long range by the deadly rifle-shooting of the Boers. Young men should

be spending more time as marksmen and less on the playing-fields. So he wrote his famous but often misunderstood line:

. . . the flannelled fools at the wicket or the muddied oafs at the goals.

He did not despise cricket and football. His letters to his son at boarding school inquired eagerly about his chances of getting picked for the Eleven. Kipling was only anxious that games should not oust other activities.

He was often misunderstood, through being quoted out of context. As in "East is East and West is West", when a reading of the whole poem shows Kipling's respect for both

K, k.

Men of different trades and sizes
Here you see before your eyes;
Lanky sword and stumpy pen,
Doing useful things for men;
When the Empire wants a stitch in her
Send for Kipling and for Kitchener.

19 Cecil Rhodes (1853-1902), founder of "Rhodesia" (now Zimbabwe), a statesman with more vision than scruples.

cultures and his conviction that the gap can be bridged. The "lesser breeds without the law" to which he refers in the poem, are not (George Orwell pointed out) the coloured peoples but the new forces of nationalism in Europe – Germany especially – where he felt that the civilized values of order and self-restraint had not yet been established. He used "white man" not with colour prejudice but as a convenient term to embrace both British and Americans, the two peoples who at that date had the technical and economic resources needed for the development of the modern world.

Kipling was already a celebrity when Edward VII came to the throne, and the Edwardian decade saw the full flowering of his talents. Along with his public life and propaganda and his constant travels abroad he kept up a steady flow of books and poems, including such children's classics as *Just So Stories* and *Puck of Pook's Hill*, in which the modern children Una and Dan were based on his own Elsie and John. He was a devoted father. The death of his elder daughter, Josephine, in 1899, had been a crushing blow.

Another such tragedy was to come. His letters to John, published long afterwards in *O Beloved Kids*, are a moving indication of what the boy meant to him. He had planned a naval career for him and the great Admiral Fisher had offered to nominate him personally for a cadetship. But John, like his father, had poor eyesight, needed spectacles, and would never have passed his medical test. When the war with Germany began, it looked as though this defect would debar him even from the army. Now came the tragic irony. It was the proud, patriotic father who, thanks to his national eminence, was able to pull strings at the War Office. John was commissioned in the Irish Guards and, after chafing impatiently in England until his eighteenth birthday, was posted to the front in August, 1915. By the end of September he was reported "wounded and missing" at the Battle of Loos, and was never seen again.

So for Rudyard Kipling, as for so many others, the war spelt – in a most personal and poignant sense – the end of an era.

John Arbuthnot Fisher (1841-1920)

I entered the Navy penniless, friendless and forlorn. I have had to fight like hell, and fighting like hell has made me what I am.

Those words were typical of Admiral "Jacky" Fisher, darling of the seamen, scourge of his enemies in high places and a key figure in maintaining Britain as a world power in the early twentieth century.

He became Lord Fisher, but he was born humbly enough – in Ceylon – the son of a junior army officer who turned, not very profitably, to coffee-planting. Jack was sent to England at the age of six to be brought up by his godmother, and never saw his father again. At thirteen-and-a-half he was accepted by the navy as a cadet, a simple procedure as he often recalled:

I wrote out the Lord's Prayer and the doctor made me jump over a chair naked, and I was given a glass of sherry.

He was posted to Portsmouth, to Nelson's old flagship, the *Victory*. There was something fitting about that. Almost 50 years after Trafalgar, life in the navy was little changed. For another half century it would continue much the same, except that, gradually, sail would be replaced by steam and armour-plating would be introduced. After Napoleon, Britain was never challenged again at sea. People assumed that this supremacy would last for ever.

Fisher was one of the few who were in revolt against such complacency. He himself saw little action: there was not much to see. As a midshipman he served against the Russians in the Baltic during the Crimean War. Later he saw the capture of some Chinese riverside forts, and the bombardment of Alexandria. There was never a real battle to fight.

If ever there were, the Admiralty (still living in the age of Nelson) assumed that the enemy would be the French. Fisher saw that it would not. It would be Germany. In the closing years of Victoria's reign the Germans had opened the Kiel Canal linking the North Sea with the Baltic, and had begun a big programme of warship-building.

When Edward became King, Fisher was already Vice-Admiral, commanding the Mediterranean Fleet at Malta. He had made himself immensely popular with his men. He saw no sense in harsh old rules left over from the press-gang days. He favoured shore-leave whenever the men were not needed on board. He provided sports facilities. He improved the rations, installing bakeries in the larger ships so that there could be fresh bread instead of mouldy biscuits. He won the affection of his younger officers by respecting their intelligence, giving lectures and answering their questions. He awarded essay prizes and made time to discuss their ideas.

All this he could do, and much more, because of his extraordinary stamina and vitality. He worked a 16-hour day – yet knew how to enjoy himself. Years later, in 1908, aboard the Royal Yacht visiting the Tsar of Russia, he delighted everybody by dancing a hornpipe – at the age of 67. He partnered the Tsar's young sister, the Grand Duchess Olga, in such a spirited rendering of the *Merry Widow* waltz that even King Edward, never a spoil-sport, warned him good-humouredly, "Try to remember that this isn't the Midshipmen's Mess!" A doctor once told Fisher that he "ought to have been born twins", he had so much surplus energy.

The King admired him. Within months of Victoria's death Fisher was brought home and given the chance to develop his ideas

20 "Jacky" Fisher, dynamic and drastic reformer of the navy. And, beneath all the gold lace and glittering medals, the human and high-spirited darling of the Fleet.

throughout the service. Within three years he was First Sea Lord, the senior officer working with the First Lord of the Admiralty, the government minister responsible for the Navy. With the backing of this politician (Lord Selborne) and of the King himself – whose opinions and influence counted for a great deal – Fisher could put through radical reforms.

He believed reforms were urgent. At the Royal Academy banquet in 1903 he seized his chance to declare:

On the British Navy rests the British Empire. We are different from continental nations, for no soldier of ours can go anywhere unless a sailor carries him on his back.

He was no war-monger. He foresaw the horrors of modern warfare, but he sincerely believed that a strong British navy gave the best hope of avoiding them.

Edward invited him to stay at Balmoral and asked him to write down his ideas on defence. After studying the memorandum the King wrote on it:

These valuable papers are to be very carefully kept for future guidance. What a clear hand the Admiral does write.

Writing was no burden to the tireless Fisher. Secretly he worked out detailed plans to make the fleet an effective fighting organization in the altered conditions of the new age. *Naval Necessities*, he wrote, *The Scheme, the Whole Scheme, and Nothing but the Scheme*. It was submitted to a committee, which he took care to pack with friends who shared his views.

Inevitably he had enemies who did not, and who hated his bluff, thrustful manner. He was quite unscrupulous. He made friends with journalists and manipulated the press to rouse public opinion against his opponents. He even wrote letters himself to the newspapers. Such things were "not done" by serving officers. He was decried by some as a bounder, an upstart bully, shamelessly rigging promotions and postings to plant his supporters in key positions. Fisher did not care. He had his priorities clear. Along with his geniality and fun was a ruthless determination – to create the navy which alone could preserve his country.

The fleet he had taken over looked well enough in a naval review, decked with flags, strung out in endless lines to the horizon. But — in battle? Grimly he sorted out the vessels into three categories. The "sheep" – battleworthy; the "llamas" – worth keeping as depot ships or for other purposes; and the "goats" – 154 of them, including 17 battleships. Under this third list, in the clear hand so much admired by the King, he wrote tersely, "Scrap the lot".

Mere numbers mattered less than fighting power. Alert to technical change, he had been one of the first British officers to grasp – in the 1860s – the significance of the newly invented torpedo. And, later, of the submarine and wireless telegraphy. "When they are perfected," he was saying by 1903, "we do not know what a revolution will come about."

A year later he suggested oil-fired warships, but there even his ally, Lord Selborne, had not the vision to back him. "The substitution of oil for coal is impossible," Selborne declared, "because the oil does not exist in the world in sufficient quantities." Fisher did not give up. By 1913 the first oil-fired battleships were launched.

21 The launching, in record time, of H.M.S. *Dreadnought*, the vessel which set a new standard in battleship design.

22 *Dreadnought* completed and ready for anything: 527 feet in length, with 11-inch armour-plating amidships, she was a superb fast-moving gun-platform, with a devastating armament of ten 12-inch guns, 27 smaller guns, and five under-water torpedo-tubes.

His most famous innovation was the new battleship that made all others obsolete. He saw that improved guns meant accurate fire at much longer ranges – and big ships *must* fight from greater distances if they were not to be at the mercy of torpedoes. Higher speeds were equally essential. So, in great secrecy and with phenomenal rapidity, he had the first such vessel, H.M.S. *Dreadnought*, designed and constructed. Powered with turbines instead of reciprocating engines, she could sail at 21 knots, two knots faster than any battleship in any navy. She carried thicker armour-plating too, and big-calibre guns of enormous fire-power.

Her keel plate was laid on 2 October 1905, she was launched on 10 February 1906, and she was ready for sea trials by 3 October, a characteristic Fisher achievement. It was, however, criticized. The haste produced faults which had to be corrected and the secrecy alarmed the Germans, who accelerated the arms race to match *Dreadnought* and the sister ships that followed.

How far did this help to provoke the First World War? The great powers were moving inexorably towards it for other reasons. By early 1913 the German General Staff was arguing, "the sooner the better". But Admiral von Tirpitz was hurriedly widening the Kiel Canal to take bigger warships and he pleaded for another 18 months. We can do the arithmetic for ourselves.

Fisher had already done it – in 1910. The war, he said, would come when the canal was ready. In 1914. Germany would choose a British Bank Holiday week-end, when the nation was most off its guard. So it proved. Britain then kept the first Monday in August as a public holiday – and on that day Germany declared war on France. Britain entered the war at midnight on the Tuesday, and Winston Churchill, as First Lord of the Admiralty, recalled Fisher as First Sea Lord, though he had retired three years before at the age of 70. The fight was on, and the man who had so clearly foreseen it was too valuable to be left out.

REBELS AND REFORMERS

Not every one shared the "patriotic" view of the existing order and of the need to protect it. By 1906, that year of the great electoral upset, the eminent historian G. M. Trevelyan tells us:

A new generation had arisen, wanting new things, and caring more about 'social reform' at home than about 'imperialism' in Ireland, South Africa or anywhere else. (*A Shortened History of England*)

Low wages, long hours and appalling working conditions – and, even worse if anything could be, unemployment – concerned many people far more than dreams of distant glory. To speak of the "wealth" of Britain was mockery to the millions who enjoyed so little of it.

The London slums, as we shall see in a moment, shocked a tough young American investigator who had already experienced the hardest conditions in other parts of the world. But such housing was not confined to the capital. It could be matched in big towns and small – and in villages – the length and breadth of the kingdom. Duncan Gray, once city librarian of Nottingham, describes the 12-acre site cleared for a new railway station at the turn of the century:

It was a mean, winding and twisting locality, with narrow lanes and culs-de-sac, famous (or rather infamous) for its low pubs, its squalid, drunken Saturday-night fights, and general unsavouriness . . . and, as in the slum districts of London, police patrolling had to be done by constables in pairs for mutual protection. (*Nottingham: Settlement to City*)

Even a tourists' showpiece like the cathedral city of York had its full share of unspeakable poverty along with the noblest mediaeval architecture and the gracious Georgian houses of the well-to-do. It was in York, indeed, that the Quaker sociologist B.S. Rowntree carried out the research for *Poverty, A Study of Town Life* (1900), based on visits to 11,560 households in 388 streets. Here, quietly and factually recorded, is a picture to endorse all that the emotional propagandist, Jack London, wrote in letters of fire.

What was to be done? Angry rebellion – or patient, persuasive reform? The little group of individuals studied in this section illustrate how differently they reacted to the problems facing them.

It was a period not unlike some of the decades that have followed towards the end of the twentieth century. There were rapid price-rises after 1906, though nothing like the inflation that was to come 70 years later. There was increasing conflict in industry – bitter and sometimes violent strikes of miners, railwaymen, dockers, engineers, cotton-spinners, and others. Sometimes the troops were called out to keep order. Leaflets were distributed to them, headed "Don't Shoot!", and one strike-leader, Tom Mann, went to prison for sedition after reading it aloud at public meetings. New members flocked to join the trade unions. Between 1910 and 1914 the total membership rose from 2,369,067 to 3,918,809.

As in our own day there were some who put their faith in strikes and similar "industrial action" while others held that changes should come by laws passed in Parliament. Some, like the radical Liberal leaders, would have been indignant if they had been thought any less patriotic than their opponents: they loved their country just as much, they merely wanted to remove its faults. Others – socialist idealists – would have scorned the name of "patriot", for their dream was international, the "brotherhood of Man", and their banner not the Union Jack but the Red Flag.

No struggle was fiercer than that of women for the right to vote. Even members of the same family, like the Pankhurst ladies, differed over militant and illegal tactics as opposed to lawful campaigning. But, notable "rebels and reformers" though they were, their particular struggle is better kept for the section on outstanding women of the era.

Jack London (1876-1916)

In contrast with the pomp and circumstance, the legendary elegance of Edwardian society, was a sombre abyss of poverty. It is vividly described, with a bitter and hot indignation, by a young American observer, Jack London, in *The People of the Abyss*, which he later declared was the book he loved most, for no other had taken so much of his heart and tears.

Jack – as it is simplest to call him – was not easily shocked. Twenty-six when he first came to London, he had already had a full life of hardships. Born in poverty in San Francisco, he had known unemployment and a series of casual jobs. He had been a hobo, perilously "riding the rails" across America without a ticket. He had been imprisoned as a vagrant, he had hunted seals off the coast of Siberia, he had taken part in the Klondyke gold rush. Then, self-educated by voracious reading, he had found himself as a writer. Today he is remembered chiefly for his tales of the northern wilderness, *White Fang* and *The Call of the Wild*, and his prophetic novel of Fascism, *The Iron Heel*, written as early as 1908.

In 1902 he sailed from America to report on conditions in South Africa, where the war had just ended. He decided to travel via London, allowing a day or two to see the celebrations of Edward VII's coronation, postponed from June to August because of the King's sudden illness. But the South African commission was abruptly cancelled, so that he stayed on in London for seven weeks, writing a book he had already discussed with his publisher about life in the notorious London slums.

He knew that people would not talk to him freely if he looked too prosperous, so he called a hansom cab and told the driver to take him to the East End, watch out for an old clothes shop, and drive round the next corner and set him down. Arriving thus in Stepney he was able to equip himself with "a pair of stout though well-worn trousers, a frayed jacket with one remaining button . . . a thin leather belt, and a very dirty cloth cap". In this disguise he set out next day with only a few shillings in his pocket and, for emergencies, a gold sovereign (worth a pound) stitched into the armpit of his stoker's singlet. For a stoker he had decided to be, an American stoker (since he could not disguise his accent) who had lost his ship.

His need now was for a fixed base.

While living, eating and sleeping with the people of the East End, it was my intention to have a port of refuge, not too far distant, into which I could run now and again to assure myself that good clothes and cleanliness still existed. Also in such port I could receive my mail, work up my notes, and sally forth occasionally in changed garb to civilization. But this involved a dilemma. A lodging where my property would be safe implied a landlady apt to be suspicious of a gentleman leading a double life; while a landlady who would not bother her head over the double life of her lodgers would imply lodgings where property was unsafe. To avoid the dilemma . . . brought me to Johnny Upright.

"Johnny Upright" was the nickname of a

23 Jack London in the guise of an unemployed American seaman, to make him acceptable to the down-and-outs of the East End.

detective, given him almost affectionately by the criminals among whom he had lived and worked for 30 years. His house was one of the modest, decent little houses "in a street that would be considered very mean in America, but a veritable oasis in the desert of East London". After a rather jolly meal with his wife and two pretty daughters, Jack was taken along the street to a very similar house, where, being vouched for by Johnny Upright, he was able to rent a tiny room. By the time he had added a table for his typewriter he had scarcely space to turn round. But after he had walked for miles, pretending to be still in search of accommodation, he realized that his quarters were palatial. Most householders crowded their own family into one or two rooms and let the others. Often three men, strangers to each other, would share a room. As for finding a

whole house vacant to rent, there was not a hope. His new landlady explained why her own street was unusual in that run-down neighbourhood.

"All the other streets were like this eight or ten years ago, and all the people were very respectable. But the others have driven our kind out. . . . You see, sir, our kind are not used to crowding in the way the others do. The others, the foreigners and lower-class people, can get five and six families into this house, where we only get one. So they can pay more rent for the house than we can afford. It is shocking, sir; and just to think, only a few years ago all this neighbourhood was just as nice as it could be."

Johnny Upright confirmed what she said. In two years his own lease would expire. His house would be sold to a "money breeder", a property speculator who would enlarge it for letting and build a sweat-shop on the patch of back garden where a grape-vine still grew. It was the same tale everywhere. "Bank, factory, hotel, and office building must go up," Jack noted, and the ever-increasing population crowded closer and closer. The "foreigners" of 1902 were often Eastern Europeans, particularly Russian and Polish Jews fleeing from the persecution of the Tsarist government. They were easy victims for unscrupulous exploitation. The "sweat-shops", where they worked long hours under appallingly unhealthy conditions, were especially common in the clothing industry.

Jack did not rely solely on his own impressions, hurriedly gathered over a short period. He collected newspaper clippings, inquest and court reports, statements in debates of the London County Council, and statistics from Royal Commissions. He quotes a census made by the parish priest in Spitalfields:

In one alley there are ten houses – fifty-one rooms, nearly all about eight feet by nine feet – and 254 people. . . . In one house with eight rooms are 45 people.

The law demanded that each person should

have 400 cubic feet of living space, but in London 900,000 people were existing below this minimum.

As for sweated labour he cites a letter to a police-court missionary from a woman slaving to support herself and her invalid husband:

Having read what you said about poor women working fourteen hours a day for ten shillings per week, I beg to state my case. I am a tie-maker, who, after working all the week, cannot earn more than five shillings . . .

His own first-hand experiences, as he went about in his ragged disguise, give the book its fiery indignation. He spent two nights in the Whitechapel workhouse, where the desperate homeless queued from three o'clock in the afternoon until six in the evening when the doors opened. They supped on bread and skilly (coarse meal mixed with water) in a dark

25 Some of Jack's fellow-guests at the Salvation Army barracks. He took this snapshot himself with one of the portable cameras that were now coming into use.

24 Many men, if they had money at all, preferred a cheap private lodging – even a sordid "doss-house" – to a charitable institution.

and smelly basement. The beds were narrow strips of canvas slung from iron rails. A bath was compulsory. Jack was "certain that . . . twenty-two of us washed in the same water". After a breakfast of more bread and skilly they all paid for their night's lodgings by doing forced labour, Jack being sent across the street to the local hospital for the task of refuse-removal.

For the homeless there were two alternatives to the workhouse – paying for a bed in a privately run doss-house or "carrying the banner", slang for walking the streets all night. Jack tried this. He found that it meant quite literally walking, for it was against the law to sleep out, and, even if you found a sheltered corner in which to huddle, a patrolling policeman would quickly move you on. You made up for it in the daytime, sleeping – if you could – in public parks and churchyards. On Sunday mornings the Salvation Army offered a free breakfast at Blackfriars Road. Jack stood outside for hours with 700 others, soaked with rain. On being let in, they had hymns, prayers, and a sermon before at 11 o'clock breakfast was handed out: "two slices of bread, one small piece of bread with raisins in it and called 'cake', a wafer of cheese, and a mug of 'water bewitched' [weak tea]." They were then expected to stay for another service. Jack insisted on leaving at once and only after long argument was allowed to do so.

Only very seldom is his black picture relieved.

There is one beautiful sight in the East End, and only one, and it is the children dancing in the street when the organ-grinder goes his round.

He had come to find misery and took care to seek it out. It is easy to accuse him of bias – he was a Marxist; he had read *The Communist Manifesto*, and swallowed it whole. But the conditions he described were genuine and are amply confirmed by impartial evidence. Nor were they confined to London. Even in a beautiful cathedral city like York the Quaker sociologist, Seebohm Rowntree, found appalling squalor and poverty.

The young American had hoped to find the English working-class ready to make a revolution. He was disappointed by the hopeless inertia which made him dub them "the people of the abyss". Those with independent spirit emigrated to Canada or Australia or America – it was indeed a great era of emigration – and those who stayed behind, deprived of their natural leaders, degenerated and were still further diluted with the broken refugees flocking in from Russia. So, to Jack London, the British Empire had a quite different significance – it was an outlet, reducing the chance of a revolution in the home country.

He did not live to see even the Russian Revolution. He died a year before in California. It is uncertain whether his overdose of drugs was deliberate suicide or a desperate attempt to relieve the pains of an illness that had racked him for months. He was only 40. He had lived life, and suffered, to the full.

26 "There's a barrel-organ carolling across a golden street," wrote the Edwardian poet, Alfred Noyes. Its popular appeal was not confined to the gloomy slums – this one was playing in Putney.

James Keir Hardie (1856-1915)

The harsh living conditions of the nineteenth century had created a strong "labour" movement in the shape of trade unions, co-operative societies and small political groupings, but it was not until 1906 that the Labour Party came into existence. Its founder was Keir Hardie, a name still venerated by countless people who know little about him.

He was born in a one-room cottage in Scotland. His mother, Mary Keir, was a farm servant. Three years later she married a ship's carpenter named Hardie and the boy took his stepfather's surname. In due course eight half-brothers and half-sisters were born, and, though several died in infancy, the home – sometimes in a Glasgow tenement, sometimes in a mining village – was always over-crowded and poverty-stricken. These early hardships were fuel for his political fire when he grew up.

At ten he was working as a baker's roundsman. He often told the story of New Year's Eve, 1866. His home was without food or fire, a young brother was ill, and his mother was about to give birth to another child. He had been up much of the night, looking after them, and not surprisingly he was late for work.

Outside the dining room door, a servant bade me wait till 'master had finished prayers'. (He was much noted for his piety.) At length the girl opened the door, and the sight of that room is fresh in my memory even as I write, nearly fifty years after. Round a great mahogany table sat the members of the family, with the father at the top. In front of him was a very wonderful coffee boiler in the great glass bowl of which the coffee was bubbling. The table was loaded with dainties. My master looked at me over his glasses and said, in quite a pleasant tone of voice, 'Boy, this is the second morning you have been late, and my customers will leave me if they are kept waiting for their hot breakfast rolls. I

therefore dismiss you and, to make you more careful in the future, I have decided to fine you a week's wages.'

The ten-year-old boy got a job in the mines, where he worked underground for 13 years. Though he had not received any schooling, he had learnt from his parents how to read and was an intelligent lad. He eventually became a miners' agent and helped to form the Ayrshire Miners' Union. Already his political ambitions were stirring. He was in correspondence with Karl Marx's collaborator in Manchester, Friedrich Engels, warning him that Marxian socialism had little appeal for the Scots.

We are a solid people, very practical, and not given to chasing bubbles.

At that time the best hope for working people seemed to lie with the Liberals, though Hardie distrusted them as allies. He was already beginning to feel that there should be separate "Labour" M.P.s, even if they were only a small pressure group representing working-class interests, just as the Irish M.P.s, then drawn from the whole of Ireland, concentrated on their own nationalist cause. In 1892 he stood as "Labour" candidate for West Ham, unopposed by the Liberals and supported by many of them against the Conservative. Hardie won, and scandalized his top-hatted and frockcoated fellow members by going to Westminster in a cloth cap and tweeds. Early the next year he founded the Independent Labour Party – "independent" that is of official Liberal connections.

He lost his parliamentary seat in 1895, but came back in 1900 as member for the safer Welsh mining constituency of Merthyr, which went on re-electing him for the rest of his life. One of his many controversial statements was

27 Unemployment, known for centuries, became an intenser social problem with the sweeping economic changes of modern industry. Keir Hardie argued that it should be the concern of Parliament.

In 1900 several trade unions had joined with the I.L.P., the Fabian Society, and other groups, to set up the Labour Representation Committee. Hardie and one other M.P., John Burns, had been elected under its auspices. In those days M.P.s were not paid. Hardie, with a wife and three children, earned a little by journalism, and the I.L.P. raised a fund to provide him with a small income. He rented an attic near Fleet Street, and for the rest of his life this was his austere bachelor home for all the months each year he had to be in London.

On public platforms, up and down the country, he was what is now popularly called a "charismatic" figure – not tall, yet impressive with his fiery eyes, domed forehead and beard, and with his moving eloquence.

At Westminster he was less effective. He was used to stirring mass meetings of the converted. He lacked the quieter, more reasonable style needed to persuade more sophisticated listeners. There were many middle-class, even upper-class Liberals – and Conservatives too – genuinely concerned about bad social conditions. Hardie did not endear himself to them by bursting out, in an unemployment debate, "You well-fed beasts!" He believed fervently in the class war and in socialism as the only way. The I.L.P.

his denunciation of the military pageantry at Victoria's funeral. The old Queen, he said, had been a lover of "domestic simplicity". He conveniently forgot the unaffected pleasure she had shown in her Diamond Jubilee. Hardie's instincts were outspokenly republican. He angered Edward VII by condemning his visit to the Russian Tsar (which seemed to condone Tsarist tyranny) and the King excluded him from a party at Windsor to which all M.P.s were invited. Earlier, King Edward had shown himself kindly and magnanimous, sending his own doctor to visit Hardie after an appendicitis operation, with the message that he himself

. . . having undergone an operation for appendicitis . . . had a fellow-feeling for all who had to endure similar suffering. . . . The King . . . hoped the patient was progressing favourably.

28 On a world tour, aboard the Canadian Pacific liner *Empress of Britain*, the Labour leader gets a ship's officer to show him the working conditions of the stokers.

had been founded to secure public ownership of "all means of production, distribution and exchange" – that is, wholesale nationalization – and to "take charge of the revolution to which economic conditions are leading us". To Hardie it was all self-evident.

Shortly before midnight on 23 April 1901 he moved the first socialist motion ever presented in the House of Commons. It blamed the profit system for the Boer War, the London slums, and almost everything else that was wrong with the world. Hardie knew it was hopeless – a few minutes after he sat down the motion was to be "talked out" without a division – but he was justified in his defiant prophecy:

The last has not been heard of the Socialist movement either in the country or on the floor of this House.

Hardie was a born back-bencher, a propagandist rather than a political leader, excelling at question-time rather than in the essential back-stage manipulations outside the Chamber. There was – then, as in more recent times – the question of electoral pacts to prevent candidates, usually Conservative, from winning seats on minority votes in a three-cornered contest. Hardie was inconsistent on this issue. His instinctive feeling was that Liberals were no different from Tories; they all belonged to the "boss class". Yet often, if Labour fought Liberal, it merely meant that a Conservative got in.

It was James Ramsay MacDonald – later to be Britain's first Labour prime minister, but in 1903 only the secretary of the Labour Representation Committee – who made a secret deal with the Liberal Chief Whip, Herbert Gladstone, son of the the great Victorian statesman. Under it the constituencies were shared out to avoid this frustrating competition. So far as possible a Liberal should not stand against an L.R.C. candidate, and vice versa, if the divided votes would mean Tory victory. When Hardie learnt of this pact he regarded it as a betrayal – and any how unnecessary. His faith was simple, indeed naive. The Liberals were

29 Suffragette demonstration in Trafalgar Square. Many M.P.s were hostile or lukewarm in support. Hardie never shrank from championing an unpopular cause if he believed it to be right.

powerless without working-class support – and inevitably the working-class would in time accept the socialist gospel.

He could not see that some of his most obstinate opponents came from his own class. Thus, every year, a bill was introduced to give miners an eight-hour day. It was always given a Second Reading – and never survived far into the subsequent stages of committee and Third Reading. The obstruction was fostered by the miners' own leaders in Northumberland, whose members did not want to lose the higher earnings of a longer day.

How far Hardie differed from many of his associates was shown after the 1906 election. Though he himself had to beat a Liberal candidate, the Gladstone-MacDonald agreement had worked in many other constituencies. The Liberals had won a sweeping majority over the Conservatives and the L.R.C. secured 29 M.P.s, soon increased to 30. At their first meeting they constituted themselves into the new "Labour Party" and chose Hardie as their chairman. Mostly, though, they were trade unionists keen to win benefits for their members, not fervent believers in a new socialist Jerusalem, let alone a Marxist revolution. Only two admitted to being influenced by Marx's teaching. The ideas of most had been formed from the Bible and chapel-going, from Dickens, Ruskin and Carlyle.

Ramsay MacDonald was one of the new M.P.s. Others were Philip Snowden and Arthur Henderson, destined to be ministers in the 1920s. Beside men of this calibre Hardie's weaknesses showed. Snowden soon complained that he was a "hopeless failure" as chairman. In 1908 he handed over to Henderson with obvious relief.

But he had one solid achievement to his credit. Before the election the Liberals had promised a trade disputes bill giving back to the unions the immunity from legal action which had been taken from them after the famous Taff Vale railway strike of 1900. Campbell-Bannerman was slow to keep this pledge. Hardie insisted on bringing in a bill himself. Whereupon, to every one's surprise, the Liberal resistance collapsed. Campbell-Bannerman, pretending that Hardie's bill was much the same as what he had been contemplating, adopted it and passed it into law.

Hardie the agitator was still in good form when, after the 1910 election, the Liberals were wondering how best to deal with the obstruction of the mainly Conservative House of Lords. The government had been returned, he declared, "not to reconstitute but to destroy the House of Lords". He annoyed his Labour colleagues by running ahead of Party policy and voicing his personal view.

We want to apply the remedy which was used by a Scotch farmer to a mad dog. He was told the way to cure its madness was to cut off part of its tail. He carried out that advice, and when subsequently asked what he had done, he explained that he had cut off the tail from behind the ears. That is our plan for dealing with the House of Lords.

When war threatened in 1914 he showed how in some ways he misunderstood the masses he claimed to represent. "Organized labour," he cried, "would never take part in another 'orgy of workmen's blood." An international general strike – even a strike of miners and transport workers – would paralyze the military machine. But when war came there was no strike, and the British working men flocked voluntarily into uniform as quickly as the conscripts on the Continent. Hardie and MacDonald were among the few Labour leaders speaking out against the war, and their lonely voices were lost in the music of the marching bands.

30 Hardie electioneering at Merthyr in 1910, with Mr and Mrs Bernard Shaw and a clergyman sympathizer.

David Lloyd George (1863-1945)

The telephone rang. It was the Chief Constable. He repeated his previous warning: if Mr Lloyd George tried to speak in the Town Hall tonight there might be violence. He asked him to call off the meeting.

It was prudent advice. Lloyd George, by opposing the South African war, had made himself one of the most hated men in Britain. Here in Birmingham he was in the heart of Chamberlain country – Joe Chamberlain, the imperialist, father of the future prime minister Neville Chamberlain, and himself perhaps the most forceful Conservative politician of the day, idol of this city which he had served as Lord Mayor.

The Welsh M.P., however, had not travelled down from London for nothing. At six o'clock he climbed into a carriage and was driven off through the December gloom. Nearer the city centre the streets became bright with shop-windows and bustling with people, for Christmas was only a week away, the first Christmas since the old Queen died.

No sign of Christmas spirit, though, in the dense crowds massed round the Town Hall. Some grasped sticks or hammers, others held stones and bricks wrapped round with barbed wire. Knives gleamed in the yellow lamplight. Thirty thousand men had converged on the huge Greek-columned building. Against them were arrayed a mere 350 helmeted policemen.

Lloyd George and his party managed to slip in unchallenged. But when the main doors were flung open there was a mad rush. Admission was to have been by ticket, but the doorkeepers were quite unable to check the human flood.

The meeting began. Lloyd George had uttered only a few sentences when the mob surged forward to assail the platform. The hall became a battleground. Seeing the hopelessness of it all he left the platform – only to find that he could not leave the building.

31 Lloyd George as Chancellor of the Exchequer going to present his 1910 Budget, carried in the historic box used on such occasions. With him, also in the formal top-hat and frock coat then worn by public men, is the young Winston Churchill, Home Secretary.

The Chief Constable could not guarantee his life. There was fighting all round the Town Hall, the police vainly wielding their batons against overwhelming odds. Snow was now whirling down, but even that did not cool the crowd's fury. When, after a long wait, Lloyd George was able to make his escape, he had to disguise himself as a policeman.

Two men died in that melée, 40 were taken to hospital. Few would have guessed that the

Liberal politician so nearly lynched that night would become prime minister 15 years later in the gloomiest hours of the First World War.

Though his greatest days belong to that later period Lloyd George was, says his biographer, John Grigg, "unmistakably an Edwardian". He seemed "to epitomise the character and outlook of Edwardian Britain" (*Lloyd George: The People's Champion: 1902-1911*)

Son of a Welsh teacher, he had lost his father early and been brought up by an uncle, a shoemaker in North Wales. This uncle, an avid reader and debater, stimulated young David's mind and by constant praise built up his confidence. Further inspiration came from his teacher at the village school. The boy was bright at lessons but a slow reader. He made up for that by concentrating and developing a retentive memory, so that he became a bookworm, comically unpractical and clumsy in other respects. From school he went into a solicitor's office and in time passed the law exams himself. But his eyes were set on wider horizons. By 1890 he had won the seat in Parliament which he held until he was created an earl, shortly before his death in 1945.

At first he wisely stuck to the subjects he knew most about – Welsh affairs. He built up a reputation as a forceful and well-informed speaker from the back benches. In the year following that stormy Birmingham meeting, Balfour's important education bill was making its gradual way through the Commons. Between June and December Lloyd George made about 160 speeches. Balfour, a generous opponent, praised him as an "eminent Parliamentarian".

Both the two main parties, Conservatives and Liberals, who alternated in and out of power, were so much divided among themselves that the differences between them were often blurred. Traditional Liberals, like Asquith, favoured caution and economy, believing (as Conservatives like Balfour did) that governments should not interfere too much with the life of the community. Lloyd George sided with the new Liberals, or "Radicals", conscious of great social evils crying out for action and convinced that such

action must be taken by the State. Even Keir Hardie, normally distrustful of Liberals, was tempted to believe in Lloyd George as the potential leader of the working class.

Another M.P. whom he deeply impressed was a young Conservative – Winston Churchill. In May, 1904, on the sensational occasion when Churchill "crossed the floor", it was beside his new friend, Lloyd George, that he seated himself on the opposition benches. He considered him "the greatest political genius of the day".

These two men, destined later to be the national leaders in the First and Second World Wars respectively, offer a fascinating contrast. Both were spell-binding, unforgettable orators. But whereas Churchill carefully prepared and rehearsed his speeches, Lloyd George had the natural volcanic flow of the Welshman and poured out his eloquence without a note. And he was not only a good speaker but a good listener too – which Churchill was not. This talent helped Lloyd George to gauge the mood of the House and adapt himself to it persuasively. His was the real mastery.

The landslide victory of 1906 gave him his first chance of office – President of the Board of Trade in a Liberal government of extraordinary talent, with Campbell-Bannerman as Prime Minister and Asquith as Chancellor of the Exchequer. His second chance came in 1908 when Campbell-Bannerman died. Asquith became Prime Minister, and Lloyd George moved up into *his* place as Chancellor, one of the key positions in any cabinet.

Asquith had been preparing – in a cautious, somewhat unenthusiastic way – the first bill to provide old age pensions. It was Lloyd George's immediate and congenial duty to take over this bill and steer it through Parliament. He had favoured the idea since 1895. He had always wanted a fairer order of society. His own simple upbringing helped him to sympathize with the common people. Now he was in a position to do something. Old age pensions were just a start. Sickness and unemployment benefits were next on his list. When opponents argued that they were not fit

PUNCH, OR THE LONDON CHARIVARI.—November 22, 1911.

THE PITILESS PHILANTHROPIST.

Mr. Lloyd George. "NOW UNDERSTAND, I'VE BROUGHT YOU OUT TO DO YOU GOOD,
AND *GOOD I WILL DO YOU*, WHETHER YOU LIKE IT OR NOT."

32 *Punch* ridicules the progressive but controversial reforms of the National Insurance Bill, 1911.

matters for government interference, and should be left to charity or a man's own efforts, he told the House:

These problems of the sick, of the infirm, of the men who cannot find means of earning a livelihood . . . are problems with which it is the business of the State to deal. They are problems which the State has neglected too long.

The proposed old age pension was a tiny enough sum, paid to people at 70. Even so, the expenditure involved produced an anguished outcry. In defending his scheme Lloyd George denounced the aristocracy in scathing terms. He was particularly scornful about dukes and their gamekeepers, perhaps because as a boy he had joined the other village lads in poaching

escapades. As famous as the Birmingham speech he never delivered was the Limehouse one he did:

It is rather a shame that a rich country like ours . . . should allow those who have toiled all their days to end in penury and possibly starvation. . . . There are many in the country blessed by Providence with great wealth, and if there are amongst them men who grudge out of their riches a fair contribution towards the less fortunate of their fellow countrymen they are very shabby rich men. We propose to do more by means of the Budget.

Among the "very shabby rich men" he named several dukes. 'Oh, these dukes – how they harass us!", he told his delighted audience of East End workmen. Other people, reading the newspaper reports, were less pleased. Asquith wrote anxiously to his unruly colleague:

I found the King in a state of great agitation and annoyance in consequence of your Limehouse speech. . . . He sees in the general tone . . . a menace to property and a Socialistic spirit, which he thinks peculiarly inappropriate and unsettling in a holder of your office. The King of course lives in an atmosphere which is full of hostility to us and our proposals; but he is not himself unfriendly, and, so far, he has 'stood' the Budget very well.

Lloyd George had, in fact, little sympathy with the "socialistic spirit", though his hatred of social injustice was deep and genuine. He told his colleague, Charles Masterman:

All down history nine-tenths of mankind have been grinding the corn for the remaining tenth, and have been paid with the husks and bidden to thank God they had the husk.

But he had no enthusiasm for nationalization and much less for revolution. He inclined rather to the social welfare system then being pioneered in Germany. Unlike many insular Britons he was ready to learn from the "foreigner". He travelled to Germany to study

the working of the system himself. He made a point of meeting not only government ministers but trade union representatives. Back home, as Chancellor of the Exchequer, he used his annual Budgets to alter the whole relationship between State and citizen.

Today people often speak of "the welfare state" as if it had been invented by Attlee's Labour government in 1945. In reality it had its origins in the first three years of Lloyd George's chancellorship, 1908-11. In that last year the mainly Conservative House of Lords

33 Edward VII (back view) and Queen Alexandra (facing) at the Duchess of Wellington's Ball at Apsley House, Piccadilly, in 1908. Lloyd George constantly denounced the rich and was particularly rude about dukes – an attitude which did not endear him to the King.

caused a crisis by rejecting his Budget. This led to the Parliament Act curbing the powers of the Upper House. The National Insurance Act crowned the achievement of his programme.

Herbert George Wells (1866-1946)

While politicians like Keir Hardie and Lloyd George were trying to change society with platform speeches, writers like Wells and Shaw were attempting the same task with the pen. Oratory and literature had a dominant influence then which is hard to imagine now. Radio and television were not yet born. The cinema was a jerky, flickering novelty, not a

34 Prophet and – some said – profligate, the now-famous novelist combined immense intellectual vitality with a surplus energy which drew him into a series of passionate and often scandalous love affairs.

medium for presenting serious ideas. That task was still left to the writer.

The twentieth century has been called "the century of the common man". And Wells, the perky, shrill-voiced, self-educated little Cockney, bouncy and bubbling with outrageous notions, was (wrote one biographer, Lovat Dickson) "the epitome of the common man".

In Victoria's closing years he had won a reputation as a writer of science fiction, fantastic yet at the same time plausible, and sometimes to be seen later as brilliantly prophetic. In 1898 he had published *The War of the Worlds*, in 1901 *The First Men in the*

Moon. As Edward VII arrived on the throne, Wells arrived as one of the foremost literary figures in Britain. He was ready for fresh conquests. Without losing his interest in scientific progress, he launched into a different sort of novel, concerned with the human problems of society and the changes needed to solve them.

His parents, like Elgar's, kept a shop, but theirs had failed. His mother had been a lady's maid before her marriage and she was forced to return as housekeeper to the same house: Uppark on the Sussex Downs, today a "stately home" open to the public. Wells had just left school, before his fourteenth birthday, and had started as a draper's assistant. But he was sacked after two months for being uncivil and inattentive, unable even to give the right change. Short spells followed as student-teacher, chemist's apprentice and draper's assistant again, but something always went wrong and the bad penny would turn up at Uppark to his mother's embarrassment.

The misfit boy would sit down to meals in the servants' hall with the butler and the rest of the staff. The lady of the house was sympathetic and, recognizing that he had intellectual leanings, gave him the use of the magnificent library upstairs. Her kindness may have helped him to become a writer but it did not reconcile him to the rigid class system of the period – especially when later the same lady had to give Mrs Wells notice (with some justification) for not being equal to the job. Unlike Elgar, Wells was a rebel from the start. Even when his literary genius took him to the top, he still carried a chip on his shoulder.

The snobbery might be sickening but there was a surprising fluidity in the more intelligent circles of society. To real talent many doors were open. By 1902 the young science-fiction writer was a member of the Coefficients, a select dining club limited to a dozen, meeting monthly for discussion. It had been started by a civil servant, Sidney Webb, and his wife Beatrice, the intellectual pioneers of the Labour movement, but the members included men of such diverse opinions as Balfour and Bertrand Russell, the philosopher, and the future Liberal foreign secretary, Edward Grey. These were not men to suffer fools gladly. They welcomed Wells for his stimulating and original ideas. His accent and origins did not matter.

Throughout the nation as a whole there was a disposition for discussion and change, a curiosity about the future. The popularity of Wells's early novels demonstrated that. His scientific education had been sketchy. He had managed to win a scholarship to the Royal College of Science in London, but he had dissipated his energies in too many other fields – writing and socialism and sex. A little later, as he admitted in his autobiography, "I meant now to get in all the minor and incidental love adventures I could". But, though all these distractions did nothing to help him in his studies, he knew what science was *about*, and had an imaginative grasp of its possibilities. Thus, chancing to pick up Frederick Soddy's *Interpretation of Radium*, published in 1904, he was inspired to write *The World Set Free*, which prophesied the splitting of the atom and a bomb that would terminate a world war.

Wells was by now a prosperous author and a public figure. He had deserted his first wife,

married another, and lived in an impressive house on the cliffs near Folkestone with gardens sweeping down to the beach. He frankly enjoyed his material and social success. As Anthony West wrote in *H.G. Wells: Aspects of A Life* :

He had formed his personal style in the first ten years of the century and he came through the late thirties and into the forties in the guise of an Edwardian big shot, neatly tailored and well-hatted, with homburgs with braided brims in the wintertime and spotless panamas in the height of the summer.

He might also have been seen in tweed cap and knickerbockers on his bicycle – for this was the golden age of the bicycle and there were as yet few cars on the road. Even the dignified Henry James would come over on his bicycle to visit Wells.

Despite his new way of life Wells remained in revolt against the existing order and committed to fundamental social change. A year after drawing him into the Coefficients, the Webbs recruited him into the Fabian Society. This was an idealistic, mainly middle-class body which sought to work for socialism – for the transfer of land and capital to the community – by gradual methods, and which was named after the notoriously cautious general, Fabius, in ancient Rome.

Their methods indeed proved too gradual, too cautious, for Wells's aggressive nature. He wanted this cosy little group transformed into a mass movement. He talked bluntly to one of their gatherings:

Measure with your eye this little meeting, this little hall. Look at that little stall of not very powerful tracts. Think of the scattered members, one here, one there. Then go out into the Strand. Note the size of the buildings and business places, note the glare of the advertisements, note the abundance of traffic and the multitudes of people. That is the world whose very foundations you are attempting to change. How does this little dribble of activities look then? . . . Such a programme as I am now putting before

35 Rebecca West, herself later a famous writer, with whom Wells had one of his most serious affairs. Their son, Anthony West (born 1914), wrote of his father in *H.G. Wells: Aspects of a Life*, published in 1984.

you ought to carry our number up towards ten thousand within a year or so.

This kind of plain speaking did not make him popular. Wells wanted to change the Society and the Society did not want to change. In the most autobiographical of his novels, *Tono-Bungay* (1909), the hero's uncle bursts out against the suburban mentality:

"They've no capacity for ideas. They don't catch on; no Jump about the place, no Life. Live ! – they trickle, and what one has to do here is trickle too – Zzzzzz. It doesn't suit me. I'm the cascading sort."

Wells's dreams of a mass movement were more appropriate to the new Labour Party itself, to which the Fabian Society was just a small but influential, intellectual appendage. But Wells would have been no more at home in a mass organization based on equality, for, like his fellow Fabians, he was an elitist. Well aware of his mental superiority, he wanted to benefit mankind in *his* way, not submit himself to policies voted for by a misguided, muddle-headed majority. His book, *A Modern Utopia* (1905), is rational, benevolent but fundamentally undemocratic, taking a poor view of the average man and conceiving a future society run by a dedicated minority of leaders or "samurai".

For several years he struggled to change the Fabian Society. Once he resigned from the executive in disgust, but in 1908 accepted re-election. When the final break came it was over a quite different issue.

The Edwardian intellectuals were by no means concerned only with political questions. Sexual equality – and sexual freedom – provoked increasing discussion as Victorian taboos were eroded and contraception (though still almost unmentionable) spread, particularly through the middle classes. The whole institution of marriage was being questioned. Among the works Wells wrote for the Fabian Society was *Socialism and Marriage*, and the same year, 1908, saw the production of a play, *Getting Married*, by his fellow Fabian, Bernard Shaw.

36 Amber Reeves, the real-life model for the fictitious Ann Veronica. Somehow she managed to combine a secret association with Wells and her course at Cambridge, where she won a "double first" in (quaintly enough) Moral Science.

But the Fabians themselves differed considerably in their attitudes.

Wells himself was continually involved in passionate affairs. So was his Fabian friend and near neighbour, the monocled Hubert Bland, whose house at Dymchurch was full of lively sons and daughters. Some were his children by his long-suffering wife, the writer E. Nesbit, remembered now for *The Railway Children* and many other popular classics. Others were the product of his extra-marital adventures. Mrs Bland herself had many years earlier been much attracted to Shaw. But Shaw, though enjoying many close friendships with women, recoiled from physical passion and preferred a sort of lively intellectual flirtation, in which he would as soon exchange letters as meet face to face. Wells was very different. Sexual satisfaction was to him a paramount need, and easily available because he was attractive to women. Even in the Bland household one of the young daughters became infatuated with him.

The austere Mr and Mrs Webb did not feel that the Fabian Society was helped by the scandalous goings-on of members like Wells and Bland, although Beatrice perhaps had a sneaking sympathy. In 1906 she complained that Wells's book, *In the Days of the Comet*, "ends with a glowing anticipation of promiscuity in sexual relationships" In her diary she noted:

Friendship between particular men and women has an enormous educational value to both (especially to the woman) . . . you do not as a matter of fact get to know any man thoroughly except as his beloved and his lover – if you could have been the beloved of the dozen ablest men you have known it would have greatly extended your knowledge of human nature and human affairs. . . . But there remains the question

37 The respectable family man: Wells with his tolerant second wife, Jane, and their two sons, at Spade House, the seaside home – "handsome, impressive and bang up-to-date" – which proclaimed his best-seller status.

whether, with all the perturbation caused by such intimacies, you would have any brain left to think with? I know that I should not.

Shaw, constantly at odds with Wells, rebuked him for his brief entanglement with Bland's daughter. Wells retorted that Shaw was "an unmitigated middle-Victorian ass". But the big trouble arose from Wells's novel, *Ann Veronica*, written about this time, 1908. Ann is a "modern girl" of that period, active in the suffrage campaign to win votes for women. Wells, as he revised the novel, inserted the dramatic episode of the Suffragettes' raid on the House of Commons, carried out a month or two before. Ann, besides getting herself

arrested, has committed earlier offences – defying her pompous father, leaving home, and having an affair with a biology tutor at her college. Wells's publisher rejected the novel. When another firm brought it out, the *Spectator* called it a "poisonous book . . . capable of poisoning the minds of those who read it". Wells was widely denounced. Many Fabians were not sorry to lose such an embarrassing fellow member.

He did not care. He went on his way unrepentant in his public and his private life. He might scandalize many, but there were countless others – especially the young – whom he stimulated and converted. Then, and for many years afterwards, he was the supreme popularizer, communicating the fresh ideas and knowledge which excited him. He had now a world-wide public. Perhaps no other individual did more to shape the outlook of the new generation growing up into the new century.

38 Though devoted to the ideals of world peace, Wells always found a strange fascination in war. He devised elaborate "war games" which he loved to play with his men friends, deploying toy soldiers according to precise rules.

In *Tono-Bungay*, published in the same year as *Ann Veronica*, he compared the Edwardian scene to a ripe autumn countryside, unconscious of the coming winter:

It is like an early day in a fine October. The hand of change rests on it all, unfelt, unseen; resting for a while, as it were half reluctantly, before it grips and ends the thing for ever. One frost and the whole face of things will be bare, links snap, patience end, our fine foliage of pretences lie glowing in the mire.

That frost came five years later, and the mire was the shell-churned mud of No Man's Land.

George Bernard Shaw (1856-1950)

Shaw was a phenomenon that, by all the laws of probability, should never have occurred. This was well argued in a letter once received by his friend Edith Nesbit:

"Have you ever considered . . . how utterly impossible it is that Shaw of Dublin could have written his wonderful plays? . . . Shaw was an utterly ignorant man. His father was an unsuccessful business man always on the verge of bankruptcy . . . He was a disgrace to his school, where he acquired little Latin & less Greek. He got no secondary education & came to London an unknown & obscure provincial. And this is the man to whom people attribute the omniscience, the knowledge of public affairs, of law, of medicine, of navigation &c&c&c which informs the plays & prefaces of GBS. Absurd!"

The letter went on, using arguments similar to those proving that only Bacon could have written the works of Shakespeare. It concluded that in the case of Shaw's supposed creations the eminently intellectual Sidney Webb, "who carried all before him in examinations . . . was clearly the man".

In fact, of course, this letter itself was written by Shaw, a typical sample of Shavian fun and paradox – for by that time a new adjective, "Shavian", had come into the language to describe his distinctive style. But

39 By now a famous playwright but still a forceful street-corner orator, the tall Irishman exhorts Portsmouth dockyard workers to vote Labour in 1910.

he had, goodhumouredly and accurately, summed up his own background and unpromising early career.

Starting in Dublin as a junior clerk, he had moved to London in 1876, living with – and partly on – his mother for the next ten years. During this period he wrote five (rejected) novels, became a forceful and witty platform speaker in the Socialist movement, spent many hours reading in the British Museum Library to fill the gaps in his education, and earned what he could as a journalist. He reviewed books, wrote up art exhibitions, and was both a music and drama critic.

Theatre-going led him gradually to the right road for the expression of his genius. He did not much like the late Victorian theatre. It was dominated by Sir Henry Irving, who, when not playing Shakespeare, wasted his gifts in mediocre melodrama. After the tragic disgrace and fall of the inimitable Oscar Wilde the new plays being written were mainly "drawing-room comedies", which diverted the fashionable West End audiences but seemed to Shaw superficial and worthless.

He had discovered, through the Norwegian dramatist Henrik Ibsen, that plays could be used to air controversial opinions. This appealed to him, for his social conscience was highly developed. He had been a Fabian since 1884. He served as a local councillor and had proved himself an excellent committee man, painstaking and patient and level-headed. Soon to be a pioneer of modern British drama he was first a pioneer in such prosaic matters as the provision of women's public lavatories, then almost unknown in London. He shocked some of his fellow councillors by insisting that the committee concerned with this question should include some ladies.

As early as 1885 he was starting to write a play, *Widowers' Houses*, but he did not achieve a production (and then only a private club performance) until 1892. The theatre managers did not want Ibsen. Still less did they want this unknown Irishman. Shaw went on doggedly writing plays, getting an occasional club production but seldom a showing to the general public. People shrank from them because they dealt with ideas, and

often "subversive" ideas at that. They were "all talk", not romantic or full of strongly dramatic situations. Abroad, a few discerning people observed this new star rising. There were performances in America and on the Continent, but foreign managements were not, on the whole, much more venturesome than the British.

40 Himself a keen motorist, Shaw delighted audiences by putting one of the new-fangled vehicles on the stage in one of his plays. He gave some of the best lines to Straker, the chauffeur or "engineer", the new kind of superior skilled servant now required.

41 Late theatre-goers mingling with early market-workers in the old Covent Garden – a colourful scene which inspired Shaw in *Pygmalion* and was later developed in the musical version, *My Fair Lady*.

As Shaw could seldom get his plays acted he resolved that at least people should *read* them. He had them printed as books, with explanatory prefaces and unusually long and descriptive stage-directions. Readers could thus enjoy them like novels, visualizing the scenes and characters, knowing their moves, tones of voice and inward emotions.

At long last, in 1905, Shaw broke into the London theatre with striking success. After that, he never looked back. A new repertory venture had been launched at the Royal Court Theatre, providing short runs for numerous plays, the matinée offering a different piece from the one presented in the evening. Harley Granville Barker, a handsome and intelligent actor and director, who like Shaw, had written several striking plays that challenged prevailing fashions, had gone into partnership with an experienced and efficient manager, J.E. Vedrenne, and the celebrated Vedrenne-Barker seasons were among the cultural landmarks of the period. Among other things, they introduced a new public to Greek tragedy, but, above all, they introduced it to Shaw. Between 1904 and 1907 no less than ten of his plays were put on.

The great breakthrough came with a play that is now seldom seen: *John Bull's Other Island*. As in later years, Ireland was often in the news, though "the Irish question" then revolved round the issue of Home Rule, for the whole country was still governed from London as part of the "United Kingdom". Shaw was invited to write the play for the Abbey Theatre in Dublin, which rejected it. It was not at all what was expected from an Irishman born in that city. Shaw was never sentimental about anything, least of all Ireland, and though he could see the faults of the British he was well aware of the faults on the other side. So it was Barker who, in 1905, gave the play its production – and Shaw's name was made.

Balfour was enthusiastic. He urged his Conservative colleagues – and his Liberal opponents – to see the play for themselves. Even Edward VII received such glowing accounts that, although anything but a lover of the serious theatre, he ordered a special command performance. Afterwards he declared good-humouredly that the man was mad – but he had laughed so much that he had broken the seat accommodating his ample form.

That was the secret of Shaw's success – the power to make people laugh even when his characters voiced outrageous statements that undermined his listeners' most confirmed prejudices. Paradox played a large part. The characters continually surprised the audience by saying the opposite of what was expected – and making it sound, at least for the time being, a brilliant new vision of the truth. Oscar Wilde had been a master of epigram but had often been content with neat nonsense. Shaw, behind the laughter, was serious in his determination to make people think. For example:

He knows nothing; and he thinks he knows everything. That points clearly to a political career. (*Major Barbara*)
The British soldier can stand up to anything except the British War Office. (*The Devil's Disciple*)
A lifetime of happiness! No man alive could bear it; it would be hell on earth. (*Man and Superman*)
He who can, does. He who cannot, teaches. (*Maxims for Revolutionists*)

Long ago, as a convinced socialist, Shaw had helped Keir Hardie to draft the programme of the I.L.P. But he was too much of an individualist to immerse himself in party politics. If there ever was a revolution, one friend declared, Shaw would not be at the barricades. "There you are quite wrong," said another friend. "That's just where he would be – explaining to everybody within earshot how preposterous the whole proceeding was."

His plays were not obvious political propaganda. He would use any theme as a medium for his message. Thus, he was conscious of the importance the English attached to the way someone spoke as a means of fixing his status in the class structure. In *Pygmalion* he adapted the old Greek legend of the sculptor who fell in love with the statue he had made. Pygmalion he turned into a phonetics expert, Henry Higgins, Galatea into a Cockney flower-girl, Eliza Doolittle, whom Higgins taught to speak upper-class English and could then pass off as a "lady" in the highest society. Many years later this play was itself adapted as the enormously popular musical, *My Fair Lady*.

Wells and Shaw were personal friends, constantly in conflict, utterly different in character and way of life. Yet as writers they might be likened to a pair of pincers: together they gripped the Edwardian public and gave it a powerful intellectual twist – to the left.

42 The specialists argue while the patient, a rascally painter of genius, is dying. In *The Doctor's Dilemma* Shaw's wit was used not for political debate but to satirize an existing institution, the medical profession.

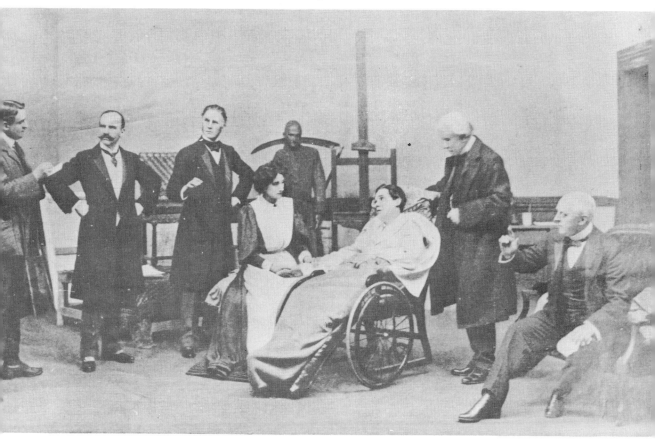

THE WOMEN

Edwardian women were still struggling to widen the breaches that the Victorian pioneers had battered through the ramparts of male privilege.

Middle-class girls were now better educated. They could study at Oxford and Cambridge and take the examinations – but were then denied the degrees they had won. Only at London University could they become graduates. They could enter certain professions, but they needed to be superlatively good to succeed in the teeth of popular prejudice – often from their own sex as much as from the other.

Though the first woman doctor had qualified as long ago as 1865 there was no woman dentist until 1895, and the first woman architect had come three years later. The first British woman barrister was not called until 1922 and the first female jurors were not sworn until 1920 – though the first woman magistrate (an unpaid post, needless to say) just squeezes into our period in 1913.

So the Edwardian girl, however talented, was frustrated by enormous obstacles.

"Home" was regarded as the best and natural place for females. Marriage was their destiny – a transfer to another home – and if they remained unmarried they were expected to spend their lives looking after their ageing parents. The Edwardian home was as cluttered as the Victorian, and almost as free from labour-saving equipment, so that it provided ample occupation whether for underpaid servants or unpaid daughters.

Women of the poorer classes might work after marriage in factories and elsewhere, having babies and bringing up children as best they could, but for the better-educated girl – a teacher or an office-worker – marriage normally spelt the end of her career.

Office-work was the great liberating force in this period – especially the introduction of telephones and typewriters, pioneered in the United States and then spreading to Britain. Female telephonists were found to be much better than boys, who proved "too quarrelsome for the work". In 1887 Pitman's *Phonetic Journal* had said:

Short-hand writing is peculiarly suited to the light touch of a lady's hand, and the graceful suppleness of her fingers, and it is somewhat of a surprise, how very few . . . have ventured into the path of this charming study.

But they were soon doing so. In H.G. Wells' *Love and Mr Lewisham* (1900) Miss Henderson declares proudly:

I have got a situation. You did not know that I was a shorthand clerk and a typewriter, did you?

Typists were commonly called "typewriters". Offices had begun to employ them widely – they were cheap labour – but they were treated as strange, possibly dangerous creatures, segregated and sometimes fed with work through a hatch. When, in 1890, one had been engaged at the Board of Agriculture, she was given a dingy basement office and no male member of the staff over the age of 15 was allowed to enter it.

By 1914 only 600 women had posts in the Civil Service. Six years later, after the Great War, there were 170,000. In other offices, however, the employment of women had spread much sooner. For the Edwardian girl it was often the brightest prospect of independence. But, life being what it is, the next hope was soon likely to be love and a good husband, and the circle was completed in the creation of a new Edwardian home.

For countless women this was not too unsatisfactory an ending. Not all of them were longing for the desperate struggle of a career, and certainly only a minority wanted to be pioneers, rebels or even martyrs. Many accepted the conventional values of society and believed in traditional generalizations about the distinct roles of men and women.

And some of the cleverest – who saw through the falsity and injustice of the established order – thought they could exercise more influence by discreet and indirect methods than by open competition that would consolidate male hostility against them.

Margot Asquith (1864-1945)

She set out to make Downing Street known to the whole of London, whereas before, she said, hardly a single taxi-driver knew where it was. (Margot)

Thus her biographer, Daphne Bennett, records Margot Asquith's resolve when her husband became Prime Minister in April, 1908. Margot had, of course, exaggerated – she often did – but it was true that the last few occupants of No. 10 had allowed it to sink into a quiet, chintzy drabness. And though H.H. Asquith, as Chancellor of the Exchequer, had been entitled to an official residence next-door at No. 11, Margot had declined it as too small for their big family – she had a brood of young step-children by Henry's first marriage, as well as a little boy and girl of her own. So the Asquiths had stayed in their own imposing mansion in Cavendish Square, with 14 servants to keep things running smoothly. Now, though, the move to Downing Street could no longer be avoided. No. 10 was quite a different matter. But it must be livened up.

Margot was decidedly the one to do it. She was the daughter of Charles Tennant, a Scotsman with a flair for making money in the City. She was the eleventh of his twelve children, but as four of them died in infancy the family was not unusually large by

43 With firm step and impressive hat, Mrs Asquith ignores the traffic of Parliament Square as she walks over to a society wedding at St Margaret's.

Victorian standards. They grew up at the Glen, a baronial modern mansion with fake turrets, set amid heather moors and hills. The boys went off to Eton, the girls got only a sketchy education from governesses, but from the age of about nine they had the run of their father's splendid library – and made full use of it. That was Margot's real education – avid reading, mind-testing games in which the whole family joined, and meeting all the brilliant people who thronged into the home, whether in Scotland or in London. In time, Charles Tennant went into Parliament as a Liberal and his circle of celebrated guests grew wider and wider.

Thus, from her girlhood, Margot learned to be interested in people, the first essential of the good hostess. Being a good hostess (modern readers must constantly remind themselves) was the accepted method by which the ambitious and intelligent woman of that period could influence affairs. By that means Margot had played her part in getting her husband to 10 Downing Street. But even then, Prime Minister's wife though she was, close friend for years of countless politicians, she was debarred – as a woman – from casting a vote. Her political influence had always to be indirect, and often very subtle – channelled through men.

Men liked women to be amusing. Many did not like them to be clever, in which case one's cleverness had to be disguised and the male ego flattered with a show of diffidence and respect. But the more intelligent men genuinely appreciated, and were stimulated by, a woman who was well-informed and could hold her own in a discussion. Asquith himself disliked dinner-parties where the ladies left the gentlemen to a long session over the port at the end of the meal. He found all-male conversation boring.

Even as a young girl at the Glen, Margot had learned to play the hostess. Her mother would retire to bed at eleven, and the younger guests, men and girls, would troop up to the room Margot shared with her elder sister, Laura. There, by the light of candles and a blazing fire, Laura and Margot would sit up in their twin beds, talking to their guests far into the night, discussing and arguing about anything that interested them. It was an understood thing in that household, perfectly proper – but very different from what is nowadays imagined about the strict upbringing of a Victorian miss.

Much as Margot enjoyed young company she also got on well with the old. She won the friendship – the genuine friendship – of men like Tennyson, the veteran Prime Minister Gladstone, and the learned Master of Balliol, Benjamin Jowett. She worked hard – as many young women did – to keep her end up in such company. She realized that if a young woman was not to be dismissed as empty-headed she had somehow to compensate for the good schooling and university training she had been denied. So, before a dinner-party or other social encounter, young girls might almost literally "do their homework" with books or newspapers so that they would not be at a disadvantage in the conversation.

All this was fine until the sisters grew up and entered society. Their first London season was disappointing, with few invitations and little attention paid to them. Rich City men like their father were often resented by the old aristocracy. Margot knew, also, that she was less pretty than Laura, but she decided that, with personality and the right clothes, she could make her mark.

She was a good horsewoman, sometimes reckless in the hunting field. She got her father to buy her a splendid thoroughbred and rode daily in Rotten Row, top-hatted and precisely tailored. She was noticed, as she meant to be, among others by the Prince of Wales's son, the future George V. On another occasion, in the paddock at Ascot, she was presented to the Prince himself, later Edward VII. He insisted on taking her to luncheon, she gave him a winning tip, and he gave her a gold cigarette case. "The consequence was" that she began to get invitations to all the great houses, and if the Prince was there he always danced with her. "And the world said" nothing very much, for though the Prince's love-affairs were notorious Margot's reputation was always respectable.

She was now well launched into society,

known for her vivacity and striking outfits. She favoured the dark colours conventionally thought "unsuitable" for the young. She liked simple uncluttered styles designed by the great Paris couturier Worth, then at the height of his fame. She had no lack of suitors, one being the brilliant Alfred Milner, soon to be prominent as an imperialist politician. But she was hesitant about marriage. For all her lively charm and her capacity for intense affectionate friendships with men, she was not highly sexed.

She did not marry until she was 30 – and then it was to Asquith, a Liberal M.P. and barrister, a widower with five children. They met at a dinner at the House of Commons. She wrote in her *Autobiography*:

44 Moment of triumph, 1908. Asquith, now Prime Minister, welcomed home by Margot on his return from Biarritz, the King's favourite French holiday resort. The sudden resignation of Campbell-Bannerman (who died a week or two later) brought an urgent summons from Edward VII, who took the unprecedented step of appointing his next prime minister on foreign soil.

I sat next to him. I was deeply impressed by his conversation and his clear Cromwellian face.... He was different to the others.... I made up my mind at once that this was the man who could help me and would understand everything. After dinner we all walked on the Terrace and I was flattered to find my new friend at my side. Lord Battersea chaffed me in his noisy and flamboyant manner, trying to separate us, but with tact and determination . . . my new friend and I retired to the darkest part of the Terrace where, leaning over the parapet, we gazed into the river and talked far into the night . . . and when we finished our conversation the Terrace was deserted and the sky light.

They were married in 1894 and another 14 years passed before the sudden and fatal illness of Campbell-Bannerman brought them to No. 10, the crown of any politician's career. But, by then, Margot had already played an invaluable part in her husband's career. Asquith was dependent on his earnings at the Bar: Only the generosity of Margot's rich father enabled them to keep up the great establishment in Cavendish Square, where Margot could exercise her talents as a hostess to entertain useful people and advance her husband in the Liberal Party. At the other end of the scale – charming the voters and the local party workers – she was no less zealous. Doorstep canvassing embarrassed her, fluent though she was in a drawing room, and the thought of platform speaking appalled her, but what she could do she did tirelessly. "With you by my side," Asquith told her, "we will some day drive the machine along at a pace with results that the world will feel."

The landslide election of 1906 brought the Liberals to power and Henry to high office as Chancellor. And now, only two years later, he was Prime Minister.

He remained so for the next eight years, until he was driven from power in the middle of World War One, and all through that time Margot was mistress of what she had termed the "liver-coloured and squalid" house which she soon transformed into a place of elegance bubbling with life. Good food and good company characterized her ceaseless luncheons and dinner parties. The famous guests were leavened with the promising young and the interesting unknown.

It was part of her effort to ensure that Henry, busy as he was and inevitably surrounded by important people, was kept aware of the wider world. Most days she attended the House of Commons debates, looking down from the Ladies Gallery, observant of reactions, watchful for back-benchers who might prove useful – or dangerous – and might repay cultivation in Henry's support. Often she would scribble a note and send it down by an attendant. If they could spare time to slip out of the Chamber and go to the Prime Minister's room, would they send a note to her in the gallery and she would join them for a chat? Such invitations were seldom ignored.

In this way she could pass on to Henry much that would not otherwise have come to his ears. Needless to say, not everyone approved – just as others were shocked by the bustle and gaiety she had introduced at No. 10, once even using that sedate residence to put on a fashion show. But, in fact, her "interference" never seriously influenced the government of the country. If she disagreed with Henry she could never budge him from any action he had decided on as right. And neither he nor the members of his Cabinet – half of whom she could greet as old personal friends when they arrived for a meeting – ever divulged to her the confidential matters they discussed.

The Prime Minister was supposed to send the King a written account of these meetings. She knew that at first Henry composed a long, conscientious record – and she knew Edward VII would never read it. So again she made her own useful contribution by persuading Henry to keep these letters short and simple, taxing neither the patience nor the intellect of his sovereign.

One might have supposed that Margot, breathing politics almost every hour of the day and knowing so much more than the man in the street, would have resented having no vote herself. Yet she had no sympathy whatever with the Suffragettes demanding votes for women. "They won't know what to do with them," she said scornfully. And when

Suffragettes had broken her own windows at No. 10, and threatened the lives of her husband and children, she wrote to a friend:

It's as much as I can do not to pray that they won't have a vote in my life-time; reason has never governed women in times of political excitement. For pure cruelty women beat men hollow.

45 Though herself a woman of emphatic political opinions, Margot had no use for Suffragettes. She was not won over by their treatment of her husband, here waylaid by them in 1908 – and much more violently assailed on subsequent occasions.

Ottoline Morrell (1873-1938)

Imagine yourself young in London from 1908 onwards – ambitious, bubbling with ideas, but poor, unknown and struggling. Perhaps with your first book just published, or your first show in a small art gallery, or your first recital last week to a tiny audience with not a leading music critic in sight.

The most exciting thing that could happen to you would be a letter in fantastic handwriting, all curls and loops and flourishes in sepia ink, headed "*44 Bedford Square*" and with elaborately decorative signature, "*Ottoline Morrell*". She would be At Home next Thursday evening. The invitation was

46 Ottoline in 1904, two years after her marriage and four years before she started her legendary "At Homes".

enough to set the blood racing hopefully in your veins.

You had heard of her, of course. You knew (luckily) that though her husband was plain Mr Philip Morrell she was "Lady" Ottoline Morrell, the Duke of Portland's sister. Her Thursday evenings were becoming a legend. You might meet anybody there, even the Prime Minister. But, though Mr Morrell was a Liberal M.P., Lady Ottoline was not one of the "political hostesses" like Margot Asquith. The guests she preferred were artists and authors, philosophers and critics, whether celebrities or people, like yourself, on the way up. Virginia Stephen (better known later as Mrs Virginia Woolf) wrote in 1909:

We have just got to know a wonderful Lady Ottoline Morrell, who has the head of a Medusa; but she is very simple and innocent in spite of it, and worships the arts.

Simple? Innocent? One could debate that. Certainly, growing up in the aristocratic atmosphere of Welbeck Abbey, Ottoline had never had much chance to become an intellectual. Nor was she creative, but she was fascinated by those who were. She was eager to meet them and, being warm-hearted with a talent for friendship, to help them. Most mornings, in her boudoir, she sat writing those impulsive letters.

It was her outlet, this Thursday salon. She had only one child, a girl – the twin boy had died at birth. Ottoline had been ill for a long time afterwards and could have no more children, and the little girl, being delicate, lived mostly at their country cottage in Philip's constituency. What was Ottoline to do with herself? She was not, she declared, "suited to good works". She preferred " to launch recklessly on the sea of London". The Morrells took an elegant Georgian house in one of the finest of the Bloomsbury squares, behind the British Museum, and had it thoroughly redecorated to her taste. At first they entertained mostly Philip's parliamentary friends, but soon, "to leaven the heavy political dough", she began to invite people who shared her artistic enthusiasms.

You made your way there between nine and ten, passing between green double doors into a spacious hall. A parlourmaid ushered you up the gracefully curving staircase into the softly-lit double drawing-room, with its masses of golden chrysanthemums in great urns. Yellow taffeta curtains draped the tall sash windows, pictures – often startlingly modernistic – hung on the pale grey walls. Guests stood talking in groups or sat on sofas heaped with silken cushions.

You looked round with nervous curiosity, searching for faces you knew from newspaper photographs or cartoons. You might well have recognized Mr Asquith, for in those relaxed days even a prime minister had leisure and could move about without security men. He and Ottoline had been friends since long before her marriage. He had lent her books, discussed poetry and politics, written her countless letters and given her the education she had missed through never going to school. More than ten years earlier he had written to her:

47 Where the parties were held. The Morrells' elegant London house, 44 Bedford Square, which some years later became the home of the Asquiths.

. . . nothing cd. have seemed less likely than that, in the ebb & flow of the social tide, you & I would ever have been floated or washed into a creek of our own. But it has been so – has it not? I don't know how you feel & think about it, but for my own part I don't wish to lose touch & to be drifted away & apart again in the stream of chance.

They had not drifted apart. Their friendship had continued, close but innocent enough, though Asquith had indiscreet infatuations for other women, and Ottoline indulged in passionate affairs – a brief one with the painter, Augustus John, who did not fully reciprocate her feelings, and a much longer, deeper one with the philosopher, Bertrand Russell, who did. It was indeed Margot Asquith who paid tribute to her in *The Times* after her death:

We delighted in her distinguished carriage, beautiful countenance and original clothes. In spite of an admirable sense of humour I never heard her utter an unkind word – of how many clever women can we say the same?

You had no difficulty in identifying your hostess before she turned to greet you, however crowded the room. Not every one would have agreed with Margot Asquith about her "beautiful countenance" and some would have thought "original" a polite description for her dress, but certainly Ottoline was unmistakable.

Yet all saw her differently. To David Garnett she was "extremely handsome: tall and lean, with a large head, masses of dark

Venetian red hair . . . glacier blue-green eyes, a long straight nose, a proud mouth and a long jutting-out chin made up her lovely haggard face." For Peter Quennell that face had "a medieval strength", with a "boldly baronial, high arched nose" and "deep mahogany red" hair contrasting with the pallor of her skin. And "from this strangely impressive mask proceeded a sonorous nasal voice, which drawled and rumbled, and rustily hummed and hawed, but might subside, if she were amused or curious, to an insinuating confidential murmur".

Lord David Cecil saw her as "a character of Elizabethan extravagance and force, at once mystical and possessive, quixotic and tempestuous". Osbert Sitwell, less flatteringly, compared her to "a rather oversize Infanta of Spain". Virginia Woolf, once so admiring but now feeling intellectually superior (and holding her own Thursday evenings of what came to be known as "the Bloomsbury Group" at her house in Fitzroy Square), described her as "a mackerel swimming in an aquarium tank".

Her clothes, which Margot Asquith called "original", seemed to others positively bizarre. Ottoline wore exactly what she liked. She might feel Grecian or Oriental – or, inspired by the Russian Ballet, appear in a Cossack hat and tunic. Desmond MacCarthy saw her in a hat "like a crimson tea cosy trimmed with hedgehogs". And towards the end of her life, in the 1930s, the poet Stephen Spender saw her walking through Bloomsbury with several pekinese attached by ribbons to a shepherd's crook. She had a taste for bull's-eye peppermints, which she sucked and crunched somewhat noisily. What you were offered at her parties, apart from coffee, was unpredictable. Champagne if you were lucky, cider or a cordial if not. Ottoline cared little for strong drink – it gave her a headache. The company was the most intoxicating thing.

And what company! Henry James, the novelist; Yeats, the Irish poet; Nijinsky, the legendary dancer; Max Beerbohm; Lytton Strachey; new painters like the visionary Stanley Spencer and the colourfully adventurous Duncan Grant; Ramsay MacDonald, destined to be Britain's first Labour prime minister . . .

Some of the novelists could not resist the temptation to put her straight into their books. Aldous Huxley depicted her as Priscilla Wimbush in *Crome Yellow* and D.H. Lawrence caricatured her unkindly as Hermione Roddice in *Women in Love*. But that happened at a slightly later stage, after 1915, when her doctor had advised her to live in the country for her health. Bedford Square was abandoned for Garsington Manor in Oxfordshire, where her hospitality continued on an even bigger scale, since guests came for week-ends or longer and friendships had time to grow.

It was at Garsington that this strange woman once more displayed her generosity in helping young geniuses and her capacity for ignoring differences of convention and class. She had read Lawrence's early novels, *The White Peacock* and *Sons and Lovers*, and they had filled her with nostalgia for the Nottinghamshire countryside they had both known in their youth – though she had been the Duke's sister and he, just a few miles away, the miner's son. After meeting him she wrote:

I felt when I was with him as if I had really at last found a friend, that I could express myself without reserve, and without fear of being thought silly.

And Lawrence wrote: "She is *really* nice – though I don't like her parties." He found her "so generous", as so many others had done, and he dedicated a book of his poems to her. After which he hurt her bitterly by poking fun at her in his novel.

It was not hard to poke fun at Lady Ottoline. But her good influence had spread far, and she had made her own lasting contribution to the literary and artistic history of her age.

48-52 People one might meet there:

48 Henry James (1843-1916), American novelist.

50 Vaslav Nijinsky (1890-1950), Russian ballet-dancer who created *L'Après-midi d'un Faun*.

49 William Butler Years (1865-1939), Irish poet.

51 Virginia Woolf (1882-1941), soon to be a famous novelist and herself a Bloomsbury hostess.

52 Lytton Strachey (1880-1932), critic and biographer, centre of the "Bloomsbury Group"

Sylvia Pankhurst (1882-1960)

At the Manchester School of Art the students (as elsewhere) argued hotly about the war raging in South Africa. An eminent visiting lecturer on "ornament" drew Britannia's trident by way of illustration, and commented dryly: "Let her be as careful to respect the liberties of others as she is in safeguarding her own!" Sylvia Pankhurst noted the remark with approval, and included it in the report she was writing for the School magazine. When it appeared, one of the other girls rushed indignantly to the editor to protest. She would, she threatened, follow Miss Pankhurst home and break her windows. It is not recorded that she did.

Sylvia herself approved of protests. Though the family was middle-class she had grown up in a radical atmosphere. Her father, a lawyer, was an early member of the I.L.P. and spoke at open-air meetings on Sundays. Even in the 1860s he was demanding – without success – that women as well as men should have a parliamentary vote. When, for some years, the family lived in London their home was visited by many famous rebels: Italian anarchists and Russian exiles; William Lloyd Garrison, the champion of black freedom in America; and the socialist artist and poet, William Morris. The Pankhursts returned to Manchester when Sylvia was eleven, and it was then that she first met the man who impressed her most of all.

I had heard my father . . . praising the brave stand Keir Hardie had made in Parliament. I hurried home from school that day. . . . There he was; his majestic head surrounded by ample curls going grey . . . his great forehead deeply lined; his eyes, two deep wells of kindness. . . . Friendship radiated from him.

Schoolgirl gush? That friendship certainly stood the test of time, and in the National Portrait Gallery Hardie is still represented by the likeness she later made of him.

Despite her political idealism Sylvia was primarily determined to be an artist. She did well at the Manchester School of Art, winning several prizes and, in 1902, a travelling studentship that enabled her to go to Venice and study mosaics. But amid all the beauty and the art treasures that surrounded her she was moved no less by the poverty of the Italian people and made many sketches of them.

53 Self-portrait of Sylvia, now in the National Portrait Gallery.

Back in England, she tried for a two-year scholarship at the Royal College of Art in South Kensington. The Pankhursts were no longer comfortably off – her father had died when she was 16 – and she would have to make her own way. The scholarship examination began disastrously. She got flustered over the first paper, Geometry, and though she knew the answers she could not get them down. She went home in utter misery, found the whole family out, and had to climb in through a window. Certain she had failed, she sat the rest of the examination with the calm of resignation. She came out with first-class grades in every paper but Geometry, with total marks higher than any other candidate.

At South Kensington she found, to her disappointment, that art students had to battle with just the same kind of sex discrimination that other girls were encountering in medicine and every sort of professional career. They might arrive at the Royal College with prizes and distinctions, but the College cold-shouldered them. Nearly all the internal scholarships went to the men. Sylvia had kept up her friendship with Keir Hardie and he asked a question in Parliament. The answer was that three out of 16 scholarships had been awarded to female students and no change was contemplated. Sylvia was already at odds with the Principal. When he realized that she had prompted the question it did not endear her to him.

By this time, 1905, it looked as though the Conservative government was tottering to its end. Sylvia's mother and sisters were putting all their energies into the newly formed Women's Social and Political Union – and all their hopes into a Liberal victory which might lead to votes for women.

Sylvia was drawn into the campaign, at first because her artistic talents could be used for designing badges and banners, and then because she felt she must help with whatever else had to be done. She was nervous of public speaking, but she forced herself to chair an open-air meeting in a park. Her heart "thumped terribly" but when the experience was safely over she looked back on it as "tame enough".

Later she heckled Winston Churchill at a mass meeting. He ignored her question. She persisted. Stewards tried to throw her out, but the men sitting near her prevented them. The chairman then invited her to come forward and put her question from the platform. She seized the chance to make a speech for several minutes against the mounting uproar. Churchill grabbed her and pushed her into a chair – she was to stay quiet and give him a chance to reply. He told the audience that nothing would induce him to give women the vote. "I am not going to be henpecked!" he cried.

54 When the Suffragettes were painting their office in Bow (East London), Sylvia used the scaffolding to make a speech to the passers-by, including a crowd of interested children.

Two stewards dragged her away to an ante-room, abusing and threatening her. She flung open the window and called down to the passers-by, "I want you to be witnesses of anything that takes place in this room!" This scared her captors. They left her, locking her in, but she escaped through the window. Her blood was up. She held an impromptu meeting in the street and made a statement to the press.

The Liberal Party was, in fact, divided on the issue of votes for women. Many, like Churchill, were frankly hostile. Others, like Edward Grey, were sympathetic. Asquith, soon to become Prime Minister, was indecisive. He could see arguments in favour, but he could not see that it mattered. And when the women's movement developed a violently militant wing he could not understand the natural frustration that drove ladies to behave in so unladylike a manner.

Sylvia was still rather a reluctant agitator. She longed to get on with her painting.

The idea of giving up the artist's life, surrendering the study of colour and form, laying aside the beloved pigments and brushes, to wear out one's life on the platform and the chair at the street corner was a prospect too tragically grey and barren to endure.

But she could not stay out of the struggle. Her sister Christabel, a law student, had already been arrested and sent to prison on

55 Mary Paterson had been addressing an excited meeting in Trafalgar Square. When she heard that Sylvia had been arrested, she sprang down from the plinth of Nelson's Column, calling on every one to follow. The wild rush led to her own immediate arrest.

refusing to pay a fine. Now her college threatened to expel her and she had to stay quiet until she had taken her degree. Sylvia had by now finished her art course and could not be silenced in this way. In October, 1906, it was her turn to go to prison, for refusing to pay a fine of a pound for obstruction. She went to Holloway for two weeks.

Conditions were grim. The prisoners had to wear clothes of coarse calico and harsh woollen stuff, and every garment was stamped with the broad arrow that was then the sign of the convict. The stockings were of black wool with red horizontal stripes, and so wide that, as no garters or suspenders were allowed, they

56 When Suffragette prisoners went on hunger strike the authorities countered with forcible feeding, lest they died and became martyrs to the cause. This 1912 poster illustrates the propaganda made against Asquith's policy.

slipped down and wrinkled round one's ankles. No nightdress was provided. The bed was hard, the pillow like stone, and as the window of the cell did not open the ventilation was "exceedingly bad". The food was mainly oatmeal gruel, bread, and on some days either suet pudding or potatoes. The discipline was harsh. The women were not addressed by name but by number.

It was not Sylvia's last experience of prison. She was to suffer it again and again, as did her mother, her sisters and many other Suffragettes. There was a period when they were given better treatment, and it was then that Sylvia was allowed drawing materials and was able to sketch scenes from prison-life, some of which were later reproduced in magazines. But as the struggle intensified all concessions were withdrawn and conditions worsened.

Six times between 1886 and 1911 bills were introduced into Parliament to give women the vote. Six times they passed the Second Reading – and six times they got no further towards becoming law. The exasperation of the militants was understandable and it began to take on more and more violent forms.

This change became even more marked in the years immediately following King Edward's death. Marches and demonstrations gave place to disturbances in the House of Commons. Women padlocked themselves to the railings in Downing Street and swallowed the keys. They produced hammers from their handbags and smashed shop-windows in Oxford Street. They attacked cabinet ministers with dog-whips. One woman slashed a famous Velasquez painting in the National Gallery. Another found martyrdom by throwing herself under the hoofs of the King's racehorse in the 1913 Derby. Not altogether surprisingly, George V forbade his household to utter the word "Suffragette". In the music-halls it became the target of ridicule:

Put me on an island where the girls are few,
Put me with the most ferocious lions in the Zoo,
Put me on a treadmill, and I'll never, never fret,
But for pity's sake don't put me with a Suffragette.

57 A welcome prepared for Suffragettes released from Holloway Prison, where Sylvia was a frequent inmate and a fearless exposer of the conditions inside.

Sylvia was against the extremer kinds of action, rightly thinking that they would cost the cause a lot of public sympathy. She fell out with her mother and her sister Christabel. They accused her of being too democratic and too interested in working-class support – Sylvia always remained an idealistic socialist, whereas Mrs Pankhurst in later years tried (without success) to enter Parliament as a Conservative. At this date, however, Emmeline and Christabel were the violent rebels.

Convicted Suffragettes started hunger-striking in prison in 1909. The authorities quickly countered this with forcible feeding, which was inevitably a brutal and repulsive procedure. In 1913 the government, afraid of the public outcry if a striker died in jail, brought in its so-called "Cat-and-Mouse" Act. Hunger-strikers who had reached a dangerous state were set free, but – once they had regained their strength – were re-arrested. Between June 1913 and June 1914 Sylvia endured ten successive spells of this heroic but horrific suffering.

A few weeks later the outbreak of World War I caused the Suffragettes to suspend their own campaign and support the government in the even greater struggle. They never had to resume their agitation. Whatever the reason – fear of that agitation, or the gradual spread of enlightenment, or public recognition of women's achievements during the war – people came to see that the vote could no longer be denied.

Sylvia lived to see it granted, first in 1918, and then on completely equal terms with men in 1928. She was to live on, championing other causes, until 1960.

58 Emily Wilding Davison, after a brilliant university career with first-class honours, entered passionately into the campaign for women's votes. She had served several prison sentences, endured forcible feeding, and had attempted suicide. She made her final gesture at the 1913 Derby, in front of King George and Queen Mary, diving in front of the King's horse, Anmer, which turned a complete somersault. Emily died two days later of a fractured skull.

EPITAPH FOR THE EDWARDIANS

Over and over again, the various character sketches in this book have reinforced the point made at the beginning: Edwardian Britain ended in 1914 and not with the King's death four years earlier, which, in terms of serious social history, had made comparatively little change.

In the short term, in fact, it seemed to many people at the time that the outbreak of war had halted change. In the long term, however, it accelerated changes that were in progress and produced others that were unexpected. We have just seen how the Suffragette agitation was abandoned, and how the war, by giving women new scope to demonstrate their abilities, made it impossible afterwards to refuse them a vote.

Similarly, in the early summer of 1914, Ireland was on the brink of armed rebellion and civil war. By August the "Irish question" was shelved "for the duration" (as the phrase went), and Irishmen of North and South, Catholic and Protestant alike, were marching shoulder to shoulder in khaki against the Germans. But the Irish question did not go away. In 1916 Dublin saw the Easter Rising; by 1921 Lloyd George was trying to satisfy the South with dominion status inside the Empire, and the I.R.A. had begun the bitter struggle which continues to this day.

In the early months of the Great War people deluded themselves with the hope that it would "be over by Christmas" and that things would "soon get back to normal". They never did. The Edwardian era was dead for ever.

The word "epitaph" is most appropriate. So many people were, quite literally, dead. The casualties in battle were horrific – for the British much higher than in the Second World War. A whole generation of young men had been decimated: countless young women lost their sweethearts and many never found another, while others were left as "war widows" and had few chances to marry again. Nor was the slaughter merely a matter of numbers; it was a question of human quality as well. In the Second World War there was conscription from the beginning, with a carefully planned schedule of "reserved occupations". In the First, there was no compulsion until 1916 – it was a war of volunteers, and in the romantic, idealistic atmosphere of 1914 that meant an above-average proportion of the bravest, the fittest

59 Pacifist to the end, Keir Hardie denounces the war to a Trafalgar Square audience in August, 1914. He lived only a year longer – but long enough to see his dreams shattered.

60 The nation's mood was expressed not by lone voices like Hardie's but by men like Kitchener, now War Minister, and Rupert Brooke (*"Now, God be thanked Who has matched us with His hour . . . "*). Men crowded in their thousands to enlist, whole groups of friends and workmates often together.

and the most intelligent. Of them, in turn, the pick tended to be commissioned as officers, and among them the casualty rate was highest of all, so that in the trenches a junior infantry officer often had a life-expectation of only a few weeks. So the total loss to the nation, in mental and physical excellence, was to have an effect for decades afterwards.

Young officers who did survive the carnage included future prime ministers such as Clement Attlee, Anthony Eden and Harold Macmillan – and such men never forgot the untimely loss of so many brilliant contemporaries, their comrades, who had not lived to share in the leadership and reconstruction of the country in the post-war era.

In a less tragic sense the war brought many other changes, some bad, some good. The legendary elegance and "gracious living" of the Edwardian period could never be fully restored. Wealth, luxury and snobbery would continue, but there were new chances of equality, and some kinds of privilege were on the way out. Women who had earned good wages in wartime factories would never return in the old numbers to domestic service. And, despite continuing trade slumps, unemployment and industrial strife, the working man would never again touch his cap with the subservience of earlier days.

A very different Britain was being born.

GLOSSARY

Act	a law which has passed both Houses of Parliament and been given the "royal assent".
Admiralty	the government department controlling the navy. It is headed by a minister called the First Lord of the Admiralty, a politician, and a high-ranking naval officer is the First Sea Lord.
Bill	a proposed new law before it becomes an Act.
Bloomsbury Group	a number of writers, artists and intellectuals including Virginia Woolf, Lytton Strachey and others, centred in the Bloomsbury of London, and known for their advanced (and to some people shocking) ideas.
Boers	people of Dutch descent, settling in South Africa from the seventeenth century onwards and forming independent republics.
Boer War	also called the South African War, 1899-1902, between the Boers and the neighbouring British.
Budget	the Chancellor of the Exchequer's yearly programme of taxes and public expenditure laid before parliament.
Cabinet	the most important ministers (about 20) in the government.
Chancellor of the Exchequer	the minister in charge of the Treasury, the department controlling finance.
City, the	the old centre of London, containing the Bank of England, Stock Exchange, and other financial institutions – often used to mean the wealthy trading interests of the nation.
Conservatives	(or Tories) one of the main political parties originally associated with the land-owning class, favouring the established order but not necessarily hostile to change.
division	a vote in Parliament, the members walking into different lobbies to be counted, "Ayes" (yes-es) and "Noes".
Downing Street	a side-street off Whitehall, where many government departments have their offices. The Prime Minister's official residence is at No. 10. Thus we often say "Number Ten" or "Downing Street" meaning "the Prime Minister". In the same way "Whitehall" signifies the whole organization of government and "Westminster" stands for Parliament, including the opposition members.
Entente Cordiale	"friendly understanding" but not a formal alliance – British relations with France at this period.
Fabian Society	a society of socialist intellectuals believing in gradual and cautious policies of reform.
I.L.P.	Independent Labour Party (independent of the Liberals) forerunner of the Labour Party.
imperialist	a politician, usually Conservative, favouring the growth of the British Empire.
Irish Nationalists	a powerful minority party demanding the separation of Ireland, which was not attained (and then only partly) until 1921. These Irish M.P.s sometimes held the balance between Conservatives and Liberals in the London Parliament.
I.R.A.	Irish Republican Army, dating from 1916.
jingoism	extreme, aggressive patriotism (from popular Victorian song, "We don't want to fight, but by jingo if we do!")
Kaiser	the Emperor of Germany, Wilhelm II, grandson of Queen Victoria and nephew of Edward VII.

Labour Party	founded in 1906 through a combination of the trade unions and co-operative movement and various political groupings.
L.R.C.	Labour Representation Committee, an organization from which the Labour Party was evolved.
Liberals	a principal political party (earlier known as the Whigs). Liberals who favoured drastic reforms were also described as "Radicals".
Marxist	a follower of Karl Marx's Communist teachings.
militant	aggressive, sometimes law-defying and violent.
minister	M.P. or peer responsible for a department of the government.
"Naughty Nineties"	the 1890s, last decade of the Victorian period, when the prim restraints were fraying thin – it was the age of Oscar Wilde and Aubrey Beardsley, of scandals and fast living in high society, and of exuberant vulgarity in the music-halls.
Parliament	comprising two Houses, one of peers (then all hereditary lords) and bishops, the other of M.P.s elected from the whole of the British Isles. The House of Lords is often referred to as "the Upper House" or "the Second Chamber". The Chamber refers particularly to the actual hall in which the Lords (or the Commons) meet. The House can mean the same, but can also refer to the members present in it, e.g. "the mood of the House was angry". Members sit on benches, the "front benches" being reserved for members of the Government with the leading members of the other, "opposition", party facing them. The rank-and-file M.P.s sit behind them and are called "back-benchers". When an M.P. changes sides he "crosses the floor". Only in the House of Lords are there "cross benches" on which members can signify their independence.
press gang	a Royal Navy detachment with legal power to "press" (i.e. conscript) men for service – power never used after 1815.
Radical	favouring drastic, fundamental change.
Royal Commission	a temporary body set up to inquire into a particular problem of public concern.
salon	original meaning, a large reception-room; then an informal but regular gathering in a lady's home, invited primarily for conversation and the exchange of artistic, literary or political ideas – and gossip.
Samurai	originally the warrior caste in feudal Japan, but used by Wells in *A Modern Utopia* for the dedicated, above-average élite needed to provide leadership in his new social order.
Sovereign	the reigning monarch, king or queen.
Suffragettes	women demanding the "suffrage", or right to vote.
tariff reform	policy favoured by Joseph Chamberlain and his followers in the Conservative Party, to give up Britain's traditional Free Trade system and protect her own industries by putting taxes ("tariffs") on certain foreign imports.
Tsar	(or Czar) the Emperor of Russia, Nicholas II, first cousin of King George V – put to death in the Revolution, 1918.
Unionists	politicians opposing Home Rule for Ireland and wishing to preserve the Union; originally Liberals, but then often Conservatives, and by Edwardian times a term normally associated with the Conservative Party.
whip	(1) a party member in either House responsible for ensuring that his colleagues are on the premises when a vital vote is to be taken – and that they vote the right way; (2) the actual notice circulated (e.g. "a 3-line whip") warning members of the date and time in question, and how essential it is that they attend.
W.S.P.U.	Women's Social and Political Union, campaigning for the vote.

DATE LIST

1901 Victoria succeeded by Edward VII.
Marconi sends first wireless message, Cornwall to Newfoundland.
Taff Vale judgment: a trade union can be sued for its actions.
Kim by Rudyard Kipling.
The First Men in the Moon by H. G. Wells.

1902 South African War ends.
Balfour succeeds Salisbury as Prime Minister.
Education Act provides free secondary schooling.

1903 King visits Paris and begins improvement in Anglo-French relations, leading to *l'Entente Cordiale* in 1904.
Increase in motoring produces 20 m.p.h. speed limit.
Man and Superman by G. B. Shaw.

1904 Ernest Rutherford and Frederick Soddy propound theory of radio-activity.
Rolls-Royce founded.
Peter Pan by J. M. Barrie.
First Vedrenne-Barker season at Royal Court Theatre.

1905 Balfour resigns.
Sir Henry Campbell-Bannerman heads Liberal government without a majority.
A Modern Utopia by H. G. Wells.

1906 General Election produces huge Liberal majority.
Formation of separate Labour Party.
Trade Disputes Act reverses Taff Vale judgment.
Launching of H.M.S. *Dreadnought*.

1907 Peace Conference at the Hague fails to halt the arms race.
Elgar composes *Pomp and Circumstance No. 4*.
Baden-Powell founds the Boy Scouts.

1908 Campbell-Bannerman resigns (dying shortly afterwards) and Asquith becomes Prime Minister.
Old age pensions are introduced.

1909 Blériot flies across the English Channel.
Suffragettes begin hunger strikes.
Strife by John Galsworthy, a play about industrial conflict.
Tono-Bungay and *Ann Veronica* by H. G. Wells.
House of Lords rejects Lloyd George's Budget; Asquith says it is a breach of the constitution and demands an election.

1910 January election reduces the Liberal majority but does not destroy it.
A second (December) election makes little change.
King dies and is succeeded by George V.
Elgar composes his Violin Concerto.
Roger Fry's First Post-Impressionist Exhibition opens British eyes to the new French painters.

1911 Parliament Act curbs power of House of Lords.
Insurance Act provides sickness and unemployment benefits.
Diaghilev's Russian Ballet makes profound impression in London.
D. H. Lawrence's first novel, *The White Peacock*, is published.

1912 A year of intensified industrial conflict: national coal strike (March), London docks strike (May) culminating in riots (July), and transport workers strike (June).

1913 First oil-fired battleships launched.
Sons and Lovers by D. H. Lawrence.

1914 Germany declares war on France and invades neutral Belgium. Britain declares war on Germany. The Great War (1914-1918) has begun.

BOOKS FOR FURTHER READING

General background
Robert Rhodes James, *An Introduction to the House of Commons* (Collins, 1961)
S. Nowell Smith (ed.) *Edwardian England 1901-1914* (Oxford University Press, 1964)
J.B. Priestley, *The Edwardians* (Heinemann, 1970)
Geoffrey Trease, *This is Your Century* (Heinemann, 1965)
Barbara Tuchman, *The Proud Tower: A portrait of the world before the war 1890-1914* (Hamish Hamilton 1966)

Biographical
Kingsley Amis, *Rudyard Kipling and His World* (Thames & Hudson, 1975)
Asquith, Margot, *Autobiography of Margot Asquith* (Thornton Butterworth, 1920-2; abridged paperback edn. Methuen, 1985.)
Daphne Bennett, *Margot* (Gallancz, 1984)

Sandra Jobson Darroch, *Ottoline: The Life of Lady Ottoline Morrell* (Chatto & Windus, 1976)
Lovat Dickson, *H.G. Wells* (Macmillan, 1969)
John Grigg, *Lloyd George: The People's Champion: 1902-1911* (Eyre Methuen, 1978)
Christopher Hibbert, *Edward VII, A Portrait* (Allen Lane, 1976)
Michael Holroyd (ed.), *The Genius of Shaw* (Hodder & Stoughton, 1979)
Richard Hough, *First Sea Lord: Admiral Lord Fisher* (Unwin, 1969; Severn House, 1977)
Roy Jenkins, *Asquith* (Collins, 1964)
Jack London, *People of the Abyss* (Macmillan, 1903; Journeyman Press, 1977)
Kenneth O. Morgan, *Keir Hardie: Radical and Socialist* (Weidenfeld & Nicolson, 1975)
Richard Pankhurst, *Sylvia Pankhurst: Artist and Crusader* (Paddington Press, 1979)
Kenneth Young, *A.J. Balfour* (Bell, 1963)

INDEX

The figures in **bold type** refer to pages on which related illustrations appear.